POETS OF TODAY
VIII

POETS OF TODAY SERIES

Selected and edited, with Introductory Essays,
by JOHN HALL WHEELOCK

POETS OF TODAY I

  A Critical Introduction
  HARRY DUNCAN Poems and Translations
  MURRAY NOSS Samurai and Serpent Poems
  MAY SWENSON Another Animal: Poems

POETS OF TODAY II

  Introductory Essay: The Fourth Voice of Poetry
  NORMA FARBER The Hatch: Poems
  ROBERT PACK The Irony of Joy: Poems
  LOUIS SIMPSON Good News of Death and Other Poems

POETS OF TODAY III

  Introductory Essay: The Poem in the Atomic Age
  LEE ANDERSON The Floating World and Other Poems
  SPENCER BROWN My Father's Business and Other Poems
  JOSEPH LANGLAND The Green Town: Poems

POETS OF TODAY IV

  Introductory Essay: To Recapture Delight
  GEORGE GARRETT The Reverend Ghost: Poems
  THEODORE HOLMES The Harvest and the Scythe: Poems
  ROBERT WALLACE This Various World and Other Poems

POETS OF TODAY V

  Introductory Essay: On a Certain Resistance
  O. B. HARDISON, JR. Lyrics and Elegies
  KENNETH PITCHFORD The Blizzard Ape: Poems
  SHEILA PRITCHARD In Rainwater Evening: Poems

POETS OF TODAY VI

  Introductory Essay: The Process and the Poem
  GENE BARO Northwind and Other Poems
  DONALD FINKEL The Clothing's New Emperor and Other Poems
  WALTER STONE Poems, 1955–1958

POETS OF TODAY VII

  Introductory Essay: Some Thoughts On Poetry
  JAMES DICKEY Into the Stone and Other Poems
  PARIS LEARY Views of the Oxford Colleges and Other Poems
  JON SWAN Journeys and Return: Poems

POETS OF TODAY VIII

  Introductory Essay: Man's Struggle To Understand
  ALBERT HERZING The Mother of the Amazons and Other Poems
  JOHN M. RIDLAND Fires of Home: Poems
  DAVID R. SLAVITT Suits for the Dead: Poems

POETS OF TODAY
VIII

ALBERT HERZING
The Mother of the Amazons and Other Poems

JOHN M. RIDLAND
Fires of Home: Poems

DAVID R. SLAVITT
Suits for the Dead: Poems

INTRODUCTORY ESSAY: MAN'S STRUGGLE
TO UNDERSTAND
BY JOHN HALL WHEELOCK

New York

CHARLES SCRIBNER'S SONS

Introductory Essay: *Man's Struggle To Understand*
Copyright © 1961 JOHN HALL WHEELOCK

The Mother of the Amazons and Other Poems
Copyright © 1961 ALBERT HERZING

Fires of Home: Poems
Copyright © 1961 JOHN M. RIDLAND

Suits for the Dead: Poems
Copyright © 1961 DAVID R. SLAVITT

The following poems included in this volume appeared originally in *The New Yorker*: "The Revolt of the Child" by Albert Herzing, copyright © 1960 The New Yorker Magazine, Inc.; "One Volume, Soiled" by John M. Ridland, copyright © 1956 The New Yorker Magazine, Inc.

The following poems appeared first under different titles: "The Revolt of the Child" by Albert Herzing, under the title "A Small Boy, Dreaming"; "One Volume Soiled" and "Colors of a Climate" by John M. Ridland, under the titles "One Volume, Soiled" and "Colours of a Climate."

This book published simultaneously in the United States of America and in Canada— Copyright under the Berne Convention.

All rights reserved. No part of this book may be reproduced in any form without the permission of Charles Scribner's Sons.

A-6.61[V]

Printed in the United States of America.

Library of Congress Catalog Card Number 54-10439

ACKNOWLEDGMENTS

Some of the poems in this volume were first published in anthologies and periodicals as follows:

by ALBERT HERZING
> *Botteghe Oscure, Imagi, The Kenyon Review, The Literary Review, New World Writing, The New Yorker, Partisan Review, Poetry: A Magazine of Verse, The Sewanee Review, The Western Review.*

by JOHN M. RIDLAND
> *A Sang at Least* (Edinburgh, The Scotsman Publications), *Borestone Mountain Poetry Awards 1953, Literary Art-Press* (Cheney, Eastern Washington College of Education), P.E.N. *New Poems 1958, The Atlantic Monthly, The Literary Review, The New Yorker, The Virginia Quarterly Review.*

by DAVID R. SLAVITT
> *The Chicago Review, The Kenyon Review, The Sewanee Review, transatlantic review, Triad, Words and Music, The Yale Literary Magazine, The Yale Review.*

Mr. Ridland wishes to record here his gratitude to the University of California at Berkeley for appointing him Phelan Scholar in Literature for 1958–9, thereby enabling him to find the time in which to prepare the first drafts of this selection. Some of these poems were broadcast on FM station KPFA (Berkeley) in 1959.

CONTENTS

INTRODUCTORY ESSAY: MAN'S STRUGGLE
TO UNDERSTAND
  by John Hall Wheelock   13

THE MOTHER OF THE AMAZONS AND
OTHER POEMS
  by Albert Herzing

The Candy-Man's Art Is the Sweetest Art I Know	33
Whistling	34
A Winter's World	35
Old House	36
The Inland Graveyard	37
Cranmer	38
Considerations of Penrod	38
Canticle I	40
Night Letter	41
The Footprint	44
Poem Written In Late Autumn	45
A Classic Tale	47
The Wanderer Upon Sunsets	49
Written In Dejection	50
Note Verging On Swansong	51
Bowery In Winter	52
The Mother of the Amazons	53
The Earthworm	54
The Needle's Grief	56
Dirge	57
Ode: On a Distant Prospect of Kenyon College	58
The Bowery	60
The Students	61
What the Cormorant Sang	63
Responsibility	64
The Spent Substance	65

Elegy for a Suicide	67
Ballade For Dying Ladies	69
The Blessing	70
Fragonard	71
The Statue and the Park	72
The Revolt of the Child	73

FIRES OF HOME: POEMS
by John M. Ridland

Elegy by the Younger Brother	79
Sons of Cain	81
Sierra: September 1959	83
Here's the Steeple	84
Lament for the Dead Ten Thousands	85
Political Poem 1960	87
Noon Break	89
Soldier On Leave	90
Crime Report	91
One Volume Soiled	94
Station Overseas	95
For a Friend at Sea	96
Trucker	97
McNally	99
Graduate Student	100
This Year Let Us Remember William Blake	101
Classroom Exercise	103
"Poetry in an Age of Anxiety"	104
Tribute to Mark Twain	105
Storm at Easter	108
Three Seasons of Spring	109
"Break We Our Watch Up"	110
Colors of a Climate	111
Whose Pines Are These?	113
Back from Upcountry	114
Beauty of a Young Mother on a Day of Perfect California November	115
Eyes Opened on an Afternoon	116

Mt. Atlas Cedars	117
The Winter Solstice	118
Elegy	121
Fallen Hawk	122
A Ring from the Mount of Olives	123
Young Wife and Mother	124
New Zealander	125
To Muriel When the Rains Came	126
Poem for Our Second Anniversary	127
In Return for a Loaf	128

SUITS FOR THE DEAD: POEMS
by David R. Slavitt

I

Sestina for Tea Time	137
As True As I Stood	139
At St. Tropez	140
Knick Knack	141
Musician at Court	142
A Person from Porlock	143
I Have No Praises	144
Comes to the Hollow	145
Partiti da Cotesti che son Morti	146
Warning	147
In the Seraglio	148
After the Japanese	149
To an Escort of an Honest Lady	150
Small Birds	151
Lepidopteran	152
On a Plot, 50 × 100	153
*	154
Blocks	155
Balloon	156
Great Grandfather	158
I R T	159
Presto	160

Chantey	161
Earth Hates an Emptiness	162
No Saraband	163
In His Own Country	164
De Bello	165
Cerberus	166
Taub	167
Meditation	168
Apology	169
Sonnet: With Interlude	170
Class Poem	171

II

Jericho	175
Actaeon	180
Orpheus	183
Homage to Luigi Boccherini	185
Solomon Grundy	187

INTRODUCTORY ESSAY

INTRODUCTORY ESSAY

Man's Struggle To Understand
BY JOHN HALL WHEELOCK

> *But of the tree of the knowledge of good and evil, thou shalt not eat of it: for in the day that thou eatest thereof thou shalt surely die.* GENESIS II:17
>
> *Knowledge is virtue.* SOCRATES.
>
> *"Beauty is truth, truth beauty"—that is all*
> *Ye know on earth, and all ye need to know.*
>   KEATS.
>
> $E = mc^2$ EINSTEIN.

Time and space, the basic components in our experience of what Einstein has called the space-time continuum, become, like everything else with which experience has continually to deal, so much a part of the act of experience itself as to be taken for granted. We are almost constantly under the practical necessity of coping with these phenomena and, for that very reason, are aware of them only on occasions. The arts offer some of these occasions. The plastic and pictorial arts, architecture, design, decoration, are, obviously, not only aware of space but in love with it. Music and literature, especially poetry,* move with delight in the medium of time. If pattern, in the visual arts, serves to reveal spatial inter-relationships, rhythm functions in music and literature to create patterns in duration.

From the Einsteinian point of view, time can be regarded as an ingenious device for a further extension of three-dimensional space, making room, by means of change and succession, for a still larger number of possibilities. Almost everything that exists does so both in space and time. This is true even of the spatial arts, of a painting,

---

* Rather arbitrarily, we divide literature into prose and poetry. What distinguishes the one from the other is certainly not the mere matter of form. To define the difference between them would be difficult. Perhaps it could be said that in a poem language is employed more as an end and less as a means than is the case in prose.

a statue, a building. Music and literature, on the other hand—apart from the physical forms that may serve as their depositories—exist in time only. The poem, for example, that you say over to yourself, the real poem, has no existence in space.*

Familiar and commonplace phenomena though they may be, time and space, like all the basic categories of experience, remain, however we may grope around them with logic, essentially unknowable. They are the prime mysteries in a universe where we are confronted with mystery at every turn. Bacon declared that "the subtlety of nature is greater, many times over, than the subtlety of the senses and understanding." † This is another way of saying that reality transcends the consciousness it includes. And here we have the key to the impulse behind scientific research. It is a response to the mystery that surrounds us. For as "the desire of the body is to continue, the deepest need of the mind is for order." ‡ The work of art, too, arises out of a need for the revelation of order in chaos, a need to make what is subjective objective, to understand and to share. It is, at root, also, a need for knowledge—knowledge of experience itself as opposed to knowledge of the objects of experience, to which science aspires. In a world of mingled torment and delight, of beauty and horror, arena of all these warring selves preying one upon the other —caught in the endless flux and mystery of things, himself in flux, himself condemned to preying upon others—man, a creature of

---

* It is worth noting that what exists in time may or may not exist in space, but that what exists in space must exist in time also. The body of any literature, existing, like a physical body, in time (though, unlike it, outside of space), is, like a physical body, composed largely of what biologists term the "soma"—those cells that, subject to time and therefore perishing, eventually become the corpse. The "plasma," or seminal principle (to carry the analogy still further), will be represented by those few works that, by virtue of a special vitality inherent in them, are destined to escape, and thus to survive, the mortality of the rest. It is they who will generate, throughout time, by their creative energy and influence, the succession of works that constitute the continuing body of literature.

† Francis Bacon, *The Great Instauration*.

‡ John Peale Bishop, "The Golden Bough," *The Collected Essays,* edited, and with an Introduction, by Edmund Wilson.

dreams and aspirations dragging the chain of his own necessities, a spirit "fastened to a dying animal," has struggled throughout the ages, by means of art and of science, to fathom the situation in which he finds himself, to bring some order, to make some sense, out of his inner and outer environments.

Every age has been, for man, a difficult one, but to some future historian, looking back from the vantage point of a more fortunate era, it will perhaps be clear that the age in which we are now living was, for Western man, the most difficult age of all. The happy and growing faith of the eighteenth-century Enlightenment, with its belief in natural goodness, in human progress, and the perfectibility of life here on earth, was badly shaken by the events of the French Revolution and its long aftermath in the Napoleonic wars. The nineteenth century's comparative peace and order, as well as the evolutionary theories of Darwin, which it nourished, served to revive the old confidence and hope, but in greatly diminished form, and after the global catastrophes that racked the better part of the first half of our own century, the faith born of the Enlightenment, while still smoldering in the popular mind, had largely burned itself out among the intellectuals and the intelligentsia. Faith in man, in progress, in the perfectibility of life here on earth, gave place, in many of the leading poets and writers, to disillusionment and despair. "Man is but a wretched creature," said T. E. Hulme,* the English philosopher, and Mr. Eliot wrote that "if you remove from the word 'human' all that the belief in the supernatural has given to man, you can view him finally as no more than an extremely clever, adaptable, and mischievous little animal." † A later form of reaction to the prevailing disillusionment is exemplified by existentialism, a philosophy that, abandoning all illusions about this world or hope for a world to come, and regarding life here and now as a necessary evil, holds it desirable, nevertheless, to live life morally, and even

---

* T. E. Hulme, *Speculations*.

† T. S. Eliot, "Second Thoughts About Humanism," *Selected Essays of T. S. Eliot*.

with a certain nobility, since it is the human condition. This, of course, is the old Stoic or tragic view rehabilitated, and these two attitudes are reflected in much of the poetry and the writing of our time.

But Western man's confidence, his faith in himself and belief in his world, was to suffer, in our century, a further setback, more crippling even than that which had been inflicted upon it in two world wars. By some tragic irony, man's supreme discovery that matter and energy are mutually transformable physical states, an achievement that placed him at the threshold of a new age of almost unimaginable possibilities for the enhancement of life, brought with it, as its immediate consequence, the threat of nuclear warfare and universal death. The day when a cave-dweller first rubbed two sticks together and discovered fire, fire that would burn the molecule, had led to this ultimate discovery—a fire that would burn the atom itself. Einstein's formula was proved to have been prophetic, and man had laid his hand upon the secret of things. Boundless energy, derived by unlocking the coiled fury of matter, was to be his, for constructive purposes, once he had learned how to harness it. Yet, in the interim, its potential for annihilation threatened, because of his emotional immaturity, instability, and aggressiveness, to wipe him, and perhaps all life, from the planet. Once more the old problem of evil confronted man * but, this time, in a form more appalling than the form in which it had confronted Job.†

---

* See Archibald MacLeish's drama, *J.B.*

† Human beings, from the beginning, even as Job, have been hard put to it to reconcile the idea of evil with the idea of a beneficent Creator. Our conception of evil, from Job's day onward, has almost always been anthropocentric. Evil, according to this conception, is whatever is uncomfortable for man. It seems seldom to have occurred to the writers and poets of our time—Robinson Jeffers is a notable exception—that there may be interests higher than those of man. Perhaps, in defining what is evil, we should apply Einstein's relativity theory, and distinguish (taking a hint from Bacon) "the thing-in-reference-to-man from the thing-in-reference-to-the-universe." (Francis Bacon, *The Great Instauration*.) There might be a difference there. Just as the simultaneity or non-simultaneity of two events far apart in space could be experienced only by Omnipresence, so what is good and what is

ESSAY

All in all, the first half of the twentieth century, in spite of its amazing scientific and technological achievements, the extraordinary power it has given man over things, finds him more downcast, less sure of himself and of the world around him, and more disillusioned, than in any other previous era that we know anything about. His anxiety and dejection consort strangely with his triumphs in the fields of science and industry, with the enormous hopes and opportunities offered by that future world to which his talents have now given him the key. Too much has happened too fast in our century, and we have been bewildered and frightened by what we, ourselves, have brought about.

It is easy to lose faith in man, in progress, in the possibilities of human life here on earth, and it has never been easier than during the period that Mr. Auden has characterized as "the Age of Anxiety." The disillusionment and despair, as well as the apathy, so prevalent in our time, find frequent expression in the poetry of the period: directly, in a cynical pessimism or, indirectly, in the embracing of doctrines of transcendence that write off the world and life of here and now, and transfer ultimate value to a realm beyond and above them. And these expressions have validity and are important, not only as an indication of our ultimate concern—which Paul Tillich has described as the basis of faith *—and of our discontent with things as they are, but because they represent a continuing effort, through one of the arts, to understand what we are experiencing.

---

evil could, perhaps, be determined only by Omniscience. And it might do no harm to apply the relativity theory to literary values also, regarding each critic as a separate system of reference. This would help, on the one hand, to take the sting out of Mr. Ciardi's condemnation of all of Whittier, except for 16 lines—or was it 14½?—and, on the other, from Mr. Shapiro's wholesale indictment of most contemporary poetry. (See the account of Mr. Ciardi's speech at Washington University, October 7, 1959, reported by *American Poetry Publisher,* Nov.–Dec. 1959 issue, and Mr. Shapiro's article, "What's the Matter with Poetry?" in *The New York Times Book Review,* December 13, 1959.)

* Paul Tillich, *Dynamics of Faith.*

17

Yet a change must come. Man cannot, in the long run, survive without belief in himself and faith in the potentialities of life. The factors undermining these normal confidences have been with us for a long time. They have, we must hope, reached their maximum at this hour of crisis. And in looking at man and measuring his progress, or the absence of it, we have to survey larger spans of time than those represented by a few centuries. Progress may be slow, but there has been progress. Twentieth-century man stands higher than the Stone Age man, not merely in the extension of his physical powers through scientific and technological devices; intellectually and spiritually he has come a long way from his primitive ancestors. Moreover, his possibilities have not yet begun to be fully developed. What are a hundred thousand years, in terms of evolution!

Today, we are faced with a challenge so immediate, so overwhelming, as to contain, paradoxically, an element of hope. A creature considerably lower than the angels has been endowed by science with extensions of his body that enable him to hurl an object around the sun or to wipe out the life of a continent with his left hand. If he cannot grow great enough in spirit to match the greatness of his newly acquired physical and intellectual powers, he will perish from the earth. May not the mortal urgency of the challenge force him to speed up the process of evolution, to attain here and now the moral stature required for survival? Will not the law of survival itself compel men to become at last the brothers they truly are? In that case, having given up nothing worth having, reconciled, almost as if reborn, we may enter a true Golden Age, a world and a future as superior to the present-day world as is the present-day world to that of the anthropoid ape. War will, of necessity, have been outmoded, nationalism have given place to a world community, and progress will continue as much along spiritual as along material lines. The fostering, the cherishing, the enrichment of life, on a crowded planet, will demand not only the utmost in material resources that science can wring from the secrets of matter, it will demand also the transcendence of self to a remarkable degree, in every individual, and in ever-increasing measure.

From the human point of view, the nature of things is tragic. To live and to die calls for all the nobility man can muster. Through art and through science he will continue his tireless, age-long struggle for knowledge—knowledge of the inner world of experience, knowledge of the outer structure of things. He may, within certain very definite limits, conquer space and visit other worlds. It is conceivable that he will be able to establish communication with intelligent beings on distant planets, beings more advanced, perhaps, than himself, more experienced in dealing with the predicament of life, more expert in probing the mysteries of reality. With them he can compare notes. From them he can learn invaluable things. His long solitude in the universe will have been broken. But the fate of life, in the individual and in the race, will remain unchanged. The ultimate mystery will remain unchanged. And so long as man lives surrounded by mystery, so long as reality transcends the consciousness it includes, so long will he strive, by all the means at his disposal, to discover or to create some meaningful order in the seeming chaos that confronts him. Goethe said a significant thing when he remarked that he who has neither art nor science must have religion.* These are the three disciplines by means of which our response to the enigma of reality finds focus and expression. This response, this "ultimate concern," as Dr. Tillich has called it, referring to it as the condition essential to faith, is what differentiates man, that most responsive of creatures, from the rest of the animal kingdom. Albert Herzing, whose collection of poems, *The Mother of the Amazons,* opens *Poets Of Today VIII,* has a poem, titled "Responsibility," with the fine concluding line, "The responsibility of being born man"—a line where the word, "responsibility," retains, in the context, some of its earlier, less abstract meaning.

Mr. Herzing's poetry, so far at least as it is represented in this

---

* Goethe, *Conversations with Eckermann.*

his first book, reveals him as a poet of moral analysis and judgment. It is not so much his themes or his attitude toward them, for the latter is often deceptively nonchalant, but his development of those themes, which shows where his true interest lies. Such poems as the somber "Old House," and "Cranmer"; the witty and colloquial "Considerations of Penrod"; the powerful "Night Letter," and "The Footprint"; and such others as "A Classic Tale," "Written in Dejection," "Bowery In Winter," "The Earthworm," "The Needle's Grief," "The Bowery," "What the Cormorant Sang," "Responsibility," "The Spent Substance," and "Elegy for a Suicide" will bear witness to this poet's concern with the moral background.

Yet it would be a pity to overemphasize one aspect of a poetry so charged with sensitive observation and understanding. A humanity, a compassion even, reminiscent of Baudelaire's, and equally implicit and unsentimental, pervades many of the poems. They have, at times, a certain rough awkwardness of form and phrasing that will surprise one by rising suddenly into authentic poetry, poetry on themes of the sordid or the banal that, by the same token, might have served as themes for Baudelaire: as in "Bowery In Winter," "The Needle's Grief," "The Bowery," and "Elegy for a Suicide." This sensitive observation and understanding make themselves felt, to equally good effect, in the outwardly lighter pieces, "The Candy Man's Art Is the Sweetest Art I Know," "Whistling," "Canticle I," "Dirge," the introspective "The Students," "The Statue and the Park," and in one of the most perfectly achieved items in the book, the concluding "The Revolt of the Child," a poem that magically enhances and increases our knowledge of one aspect of the experience of childhood.

It must suffice to quote briefly some of the lines, or fragments of lines, to be found throughout Mr. Herzing's book, that exemplify his image-making power, his freshness of metaphor: "Some train hurls silence from the bumptious air," ". . . the edge/ Of my endurance tilts away," "Tossed silken hair awry, spilled wrist and ankle," "Their long keels bevel the insouciant waves," "Comber still mounting comber like a range," "Streets rise up hissing with the tread of traffic," "This moonlight lying on the sand like frost," ". . . the sun descending, half of light/ Crumples away," ". . . the night/ Offers Valhallas for the shaping eye," ". . . concussive stars/ That pinpoint in the eyes like moons," ". . . the drift/ Of human souls that pass like whirling snow," "He wakes outside the chores of sleep," ". . . rocks/ Slanted like tables toward the surgical sun," ". . . the Over-soul/ Anaemic udder to an earth of forms," "A splendid, savage hour, gone wild with green," ". . . one whose eyes/ With swift evasion slide in a small, wild face."

In a collection that has great diversity of subject, though not of form, and a definite unity in its point of view, the following stand out as the works that seem the most completely realized: "The Candy Man's Art Is the Sweetest Art I Know," "Old House," "Night Letter," "The Wanderer Upon Sunsets," "Written In Dejection," "Note Verging on Swansong," "The Mother of the Amazons," "The Earthworm," with its Freudian overtones, "Dirge," "The Bowery," "The Students," "What the Cormorant Sang," "The Statue and the Park," and "The Revolt of the Child." In some of these, craft and technique have done their job so thoroughly as to have consumed themselves, as it were, in the process and dropped off, releasing the poem, free of any disturbing trace of them, to move on its own momentum.

There is, in Mr. Herzing's work, a homely cleaving to everyday reality that sometimes brings great rewards. A slight monotony of form and measure in the employment of what is, for the most part, a traditional technique, and occasional echoes from influences, not yet fully assimilated, of older poets, Rimbaud, Stevens, Frost, Auden, Tate, Wilbur, and others, are offset by the fact that, now and again, in these pages, we are made aware of a new poetic voice speaking in terms relevant to our time, and speaking with both art and sincerity. This voice is heard most clearly in those later poems, like "The Needle's Grief" and "The Students," where the author appears to be moving in the direction of free-er forms.

Mr. Herzing writes: "For me, the poem is in part a means of self-discovery. Although I occasionally begin with a set topic or a set idea in mind, my more usual procedure is simply to begin with a word or a line, one that may have slipped into my head quite unconnectedly, say in some moment of leisure or fatigue, and to follow it from there. Thus words follow words, and I do not totally realise all I am saying, or mean to say, until the poem is finished."

While the poetry of Mr. Herzing, as suggested above, shows its underlying preoccupation to be with moral exploration and judgment, the poetry of Mr. Ridland, in his *Fires of Home,* the collection that follows Mr. Herzing's in *Poets of Today VIII,* is, over and over again, even more specifically concerned with those questions that underlie all others. To sense this, one has but to read such poems as "Sierra: September 1959," "Lament for the Dead Ten Thousands," "Political Poem 1960," "Soldier On Leave," the superb "Crime Report," "This Year Let Us Remember William Blake." Mr. Ridland is more politically aware, more implicated, than is Mr. Herzing, so that his concern with moral problems and with moral judgment is more sharply particularized, more likely to be focussed on the concrete instance. And the poems of his that have the moral problem for background fall, most of them, into what is, roughly, the first half of his book, the rest of which is more personal in substance, more lyrical in character. The poems in this, the latter part of his collection, have, as might be expected, a greater profusion of image and metaphor, a greater richness of verbal texture.

Mr. Ridland's art as a poet is, however, one of extreme fastidiousness, an art almost always stripped and austere. In his use of free cadence and unrhymed measure, of sprung rhythm and of the syncopation of rhythm by means of the spondee, as well as in his adjectival restraint, this poet manifests himself as an accomplished, even a sophisticated, craftsman. This may seem to imply too strict a control of the medium, a lack of abandon, of emotional force. Quite the reverse is the case. Few first books, in our time, have shown so appealing a human warmth as will be found in *Fires of Home,* whose title itself gives the clue to the humanity with which these poems are informed. Mr. Ridland may be a poet of intellectual toughness; he is also a man of feeling, well equipped, by the disciplines and strategies of art, to break through the critical guard that is so quick, in each one of us today, to parry all but the most expert thrust of the emotions.

Many of the poems in *Fires of Home* have to do with people—individuals or types: the deeply moving poem that opens the book, "Elegy by the Younger Brother" ("What here lies dead is your erect spirit"); the starkly stated "Sons of Cain"; "Sierra: September 1959," a monument to the lost Jews and children of Warsaw (". . . in the silence in which trees fall, it is said, in the silent forest"); "Lament for the Dead Ten Thousands," where the fictive narrator is the major who dropped the atomic bomb on Hiroshima; "Noon Break," a lieutenant's report on his men; "Soldier On Leave"; "Station Overseas"; "Trucker"; the touching characterization of "McNally"; "Graduate Student"; "This Year Let Us Remember William Blake"; the playful "Classroom Exercise"; "Poetry In an Age of Anxiety"; "Tribute to Mark Twain" (". . . the palpitations/ of recognizably the central human heart"); "Beauty of a Young Mother On a Day of Perfect California November"; "Elegy, for Arthur Jandry" (". . . He lived outside of himself—/ He wore his body lightly, as a tree wears leaves"); "Young Wife and Mother" ("Strange, that devotion genders beauty"); "New Zealander"; "To Muriel When the Rains Came"; "Poem for Our Second Anniversary"—all these have people for theme.

It is in his lyrical evocations of natural beauty, however, that Mr. Ridland's talent shows at its richest. There are five especially fine poems falling within this general category, and each one of them contains phrases and passages that make quotation hard to resist:

"Three Seasons of Spring" (". . . rattled our plum trees/ and shook on them a sudden, soft, quick,/ evanescent blizzard of blossoms," ". . . played all winter in the symphony of twigs"); "Colors of a Climate" ("where the thin rain prances," ". . . As each green field/ flashes with the riot of blade"); "Back From Up-Country" ("Pulled into my head/ odor, and tang/ of sky to my tongue"); and "The Winter Solstice (New Zealand, June)" (". . . the night above me flutters its wings of stars," ". . . echoes of daylight gather in every patch of pealing water," ". . . the shining clatter of this moon," "a human noise does something/ in the dark," "Yet nowhere the moon echoes wholly in vain/ This bright song of the sun"). And observe, in "Whose Pines Are These?", what can be done with twenty-two questioning words, and the merest wisp of an idea, to create a mood both strong and tender. Another memorable poem, outside the above general category, and harder and more bitter, with an almost iron clangor, is "A Ring from the Mount of Olives."

Mr. Ridland says of himself, "To name all my Masters would be impossible, since many of them were stray lines and poems. But early on I can point to Auden (he came to lecture at Swarthmore when I was a freshman), Dylan Thomas, Yeats: a normal pattern. Later: Edwin Muir, Blake, and—Yeats. More recently: Roethke and again Yeats. And behind them all, like a dictionary of the possible: Shakespeare. Choices which may reveal nothing. On none of these, however, could I write a competent critique: which is one of the proofs that I have studied under them. The greatest thing a Master can do for a young poet is to produce a line or two that will resound for him effortlessly and without the exertion of will. The greatest danger to a poet is that he should become the servant of his will. His greatest blessing: to be blessed with poems, like a flowering tree (I also believe in pruning.)."

David R. Slavitt, whose first collection, *Suits for the Dead,* concludes *Poets Of Today VIII,* has interesting things to say with re-

ESSAY

gard to the concept of poetry as a way of knowing. "Poetry," he has declared, "increases our knowledge of experience, but it also shapes that experience and the objective world as well. In a like manner, the Greek sculptors not only showed us how to look at nudes, but invented and prescribed the human body itself. If I presume to write at all," he adds, "it is foolish to go at it in a half-hearted way: almost against my will, I have come to believe in the vatic nature of poetry, and I write with Moses' fear upon me. In practical terms, I think, this is one explanation of my ever-increasing penchant for the longer poem—if I'm going to jump out of a window, it might as well be from the top floor."

You will find poems in Mr. Slavitt's book that can serve to illustrate this concept of poetry (a concept equally applicable to all the arts) as a way of knowing, as a revelation, which interprets, and thus brings order out of, the multiplicity and chaos of experience—by means of selection and synthesis giving it form, and thereby increasing our knowledge and our understanding of it. The methods by which a poem attacks our inveterate apathy will be various, but the essence of them is always suggestion, indirection, obliquity, implication, never the frontal assault. In such poems as "Blocks" and "Balloons" ("to watch it nose the ceiling like a goldfish"), we rediscover with delight, and therefore more fully comprehend, certain childhood experiences. Again, in the book's concluding poem, and one of its finest, "Solomon Grundy, a bedtime poem for my son," we are offered a renewed partaking in, and understanding of, another childhood experience, but with this difference, that the experience is now made to live for us through the awareness of an adult, the father, whose affectionate, mock-heroic retelling of the old nursery rhyme adds a new dimension to the character of the experience, giving it a certain self-conscious, humorous, grown-up amplitude, as well as its tragic insights and implications. The aura of an episode experienced, as it were, on two levels, that of the father and that of the child's tacit reactions as conceived by the father, is beautifully and delicately conveyed in the poem, through the device of tone.

This brings us to one of the outstanding characteristics of Mr. Slavitt's work, his use of tone: either to mask an inner seriousness, which is then gradually permitted to assert itself, and with all the greater force, as the poem goes on; or, as in the case of the poem we have just been discussing, to yield us an experience on two levels. There is a sardonic, Heinesque nonchalance and mischief about such poems, for instance, as "Knick-Knack," an exquisite, deceptively tame little piece that packs a considerable punch; the cruel and detached "Musician At Court" (". . . how disparate themes will sometimes intersect"); "Partiti da Cotesti che Son Morti," where the violence of feeling is heightened by the mocking tone (". . . she was false as the lunatic sea"); "Chantey"; "Taub"; "Apology" (". . . hanging like geometry/ on an insubstantial point"); and "Sonnet: With Interlude" ("all bid me comb my hair of poetry").

What, then, can we say are the distinguishing characteristics that define Mr. Slavitt's work, throughout poems as diverse in form and nature as the skillful "Sestina for Tea Time" (". . . the idea of conversation with the words left out"); the cynical and suave "At St. Tropez"; the darkly sensual "In the Seraglio"; in such accomplished lyricism as "Warning," or the poem whose title is merely an asterisk, or the lovely "As True as I Stood" (". . . sound leaks through mind as rain through a great sieve"); in such portraits of people as we get in the macabre "Lepidopteran" (". . . They bear/ all tombstones with them on their pallid wings") and "Taub" ("there isn't any back to a dead man's jacket"); the grotesque brutality of "Great Grandfather"; "IRT"; the affectionate "In His Own Country"; the moving and richly musical "Homage to Luigi Boccherini" ("the color of jays, gay and gliding," "in drowsy claret afternoons"); the dry humor of "A Person from Porlock"; in poems of ideas like "Earth Hates an Emptiness," "No Saraband," with its curious symbolism, "De Bello," and "Meditation"; the witty didacticism of "Class Poem" ("the poem's mine; the matter's your concern," ". . . learning is but the footnote to the man"); the autobiographical sketches, "Apology" and "Sonnet: With Interlude"; and, finally, in the longer, narrative poems, "Jericho," "Actaeon," which uses a highly ingenious device for giving us another point of view on the old story (". . . wet limbs gleaming in the sprinkled sunlight," "who sleep through dawns, and who forget death/ lurking in sunsets," ". . . the clouds, riding/ random in the usual sky"), and "Orpheus," one of the most beautiful poems in the collection ("The river sang all along out of mouth and source," ". . . Her flowing shroud/ unravelled as her blood ran to his song," "whose head stayed tides at the flood in boundless singing," ". . . returned to the grey land/ where music is enough")? In answer to the above question, it can be said that one of the distinguishing characteristics of Mr. Slavitt's poetry is a severe restraint in the use of figurative language. It is the brilliance and clarity of his work, its brisk pace and taut resonance of line, its ironic and sardonic counterpoint, and, above all, its dramatic tensions, rather than any striking use of imagery or metaphor, that make it memorable.

THE MOTHER OF THE AMAZONS
AND
OTHER POEMS

By ALBERT HERZING

Copyright © 1961 Albert Herzing

To My Mother and Father

THE CANDY-MAN'S ART
IS THE SWEETEST ART I KNOW

The candy-man's art is the sweetest art I know
Unless the fireworks-man can master him,
Whose spent confections curl in the sky with a glow
Of starry sugar, coloring and cream
To dazzle everything—but even so
The candy-man's art is the sweeter of the two

Whose gauds of color, stacked on trays in the clean
Cathedral of his counter, entice to worship
The housewife, the good husband; even the lean
Irreligious urchin asserts that his religion
Is a wild surging of such masterful rain
As sweetens the tiger and makes fierce the pigeon;

Or holds for us those lollipops like a rainbow
Hinting of all voluptuousness, and even
That nicer nothingness one also knew
As a milk-fed child, his mother humming so
He thought (who could not think) all heaven had come,
Lovely as cellophane, into his well-scrubbed room.

But, "Heaven's my gum-drop, I'll have it all in a bag,"
The child may later pipe; till, hiding in words,
A metaphysical taffy comes to swell
The sad, decaying jaw-line of his hours—
No gum-drops then! Nor will he bear an ounce
Of that glib confection he munched on once . . .

Sing *carpe diem!* the candy-man must come
Himself at last to a narrow room;
The burly, hurling world that whirls in zones
Will hammer out tart epitaphiums
For the walls of heaven, all its sweetness gone,
And no more candy under the sun!

WHISTLING

Sudden the bouncing on some bounding days
In spring: and a young man's rapidly turning
A spinning corner from an alley of brick
—How he will whistle, pivot on a stick
To counterpoint from palings a simpleton's patter
Of notes, and herringbone despair
With ringing friezes, till its sound-waves bear
Ramified sweetness beyond furious air!

Clearly, this world delights him; and lately the sheer
Positive goodness of his bustle through days
Mads him to whistling, who may grandly praise
His sweetie's sex or twit a street to its death
In blissful noise—so boyish over lathe,
Lithe workers at their work tune up in a mayhem
Of hoots, blasts, whistles, although time's in them
Whose placider undersong shall fire their hours . . .

The wrens of pleasure whistle everywhere
And when it's nightfall, and the streets are dark,
Small boys assert their pipings through the park
Like birds, and hoist up horror: The berserk
Lolloping monster bubbles a weak whistle
Of sexual fear, while roaring on a trestle
Some train hurls silence from the bumptious air,
And passing by, wills richer silence there.

Our goings and comings cause a similar silence
Sandwiched with whistles as we munch on winds:
Unfriendly sunshine, and the hooters blowing
Where but from love? and when all's said and done
What had we shaped to have love's staying?
. . . Now whistle darkly, birds! the day sinks down
To deeper silence in those final skies
Where the very old, so sadly wise, don't whistle!

A WINTER'S WORLD

A jag of white leans downward; sudden ascents
Slant upward; fells and plains
Extend for snowy leagues, where bird nor beast
Endure the silence; a zero of fall
And spring is equally bare
Of the usual sparse herbage, meagre light,
Or inhalable air; and distance stills
The spirit now (that folds, blue as a stone,
Into the wells of its aloneness),
Where everything stills itself, by itself,
Or is stilled within itself, by vastness.

—Here the irreverent seem awed
As though confronted with a new religion;
Not even the knowing reverent can cope
With all the chilly wonder of this region;
Breathlessly sunk below the tundra below
Its ice, the mammoth dreams of aeons ago
Before ice happened, and dreams much less now
Of age and strength (it, too, is very silent);
Involved in this scene, the mythical snowman
Macerates, horribly, its silent prey,
While all its north keeps silence, like a woman.

What noise, indeed, could enter? What man
Sterner than Shackleton could perpetrate this
Whiteness and live? Must one experience
A more than breathless pause,
The silence of the diving-bell, or tense
Moment between two pauses, zero within
The heart protracted by its muscles and oils
(That struggle mightily within its toils)—
Till this is liveable: a winter's world
That settles in leagues of still intent
Everyone's fate, and leaves the traveller silent?

OLD HOUSE

Delinquent, huddled in the grass,
Small animals eye it; the yard around is
Scraggly with wind-soiled, over-pampered weeds
That fatten, slicken, die—most uselessly;
Though some, in blinded vanity, still lift
Gaunt, seedless heads: high-towering stalks
That crumble in the wind without a shift.

Such as they are, they lob an empty shadow
That falls, at times, almost on the house
Which, too, is dying, and bares its once-fine show
To the rude inspection of the rumpled grouse
And homespun mouse—till only here and there
Can one trace out what once was panoply,
But now is bent roof, portico and pillar;

Sum-total ruin where the huge belles danced,
Beribboned amazons too hot for our keeping
And men whose great dimensions spanned a myth;
In what postmortal country they are sleeping
It is unknown to us whether they smile
On us the heirs, returning to assess
This crumpling whole that whitens in the sun
And which to enter might be ruinous.

Therefore, I watch in silence; no prayer escapes
Above the house, nor have my own dumb lips
Sullied with words the rapturous, fine air
Of a day so pure that almost one forgives
The gorgeous pageant of their stately lives

That left us this: a house that crumbles slowly
And good for show, but not to live in really.

THE INLAND GRAVEYARD

So near the road that drivers seldom see it
And screened by weeds so tall that now
The pruning winds can't level them (fierce straw
Guarding a graveyard, so long unvisited
You'd think our piety were lapsed or dead):
So near the road that horns
Of perilous passers at the curve
Can't alter now, nor swerve
Their dizzying drift past the white line
That stands for safety and that checks them in:

Nostalgia of nature in a quiet place
Lurking behind; a feeling for the dead
Grass by the highway, almost by the head
Of fallen stones that mark their risen names—
Remains for you, as quietly you sink
Beside a dear mound, almost by the brink
Of graves you have forgotten, or never knew
While graves you have forgotten, but once knew
Outdistance thought. Here Holt and Harrington
Seed the dry acres of decaying stone

Forever, and their virtues (rough and humble,
Forgotten as the stones that bear their names)
Merge with oblivion. A few more fallen years
Brings once again the wilderness they found
(But empty of them as is the day of sound)
Unless indeed, in some short space, men build
A powerhouse here, that whines in steady drones
Above their bones, and lights some tenement
Where, past their puritan intent,
Life messily happens and the dead go on dying.

CRANMER

      But not as Hooper, when the faggots flared
      That wet day in October, and flickered out
      Almost. Forty whole minutes of burning. Lord Lord!
      Thy Will must judge.—Yet if the martyrs come
      In tiers, with haloes, flaming to this pyre
      It is a pain I shall endure
      For always, and my hand as pledge
      I'll place upon the edge
      And margin of enveloping fire
      To play and flicker there,
      A moveless rock—if not the edge
      Of my endurance tilts away—
      Appeased, in Time, till Judgment Day.

CONSIDERATIONS OF PENROD

    When one is balding, middle-aged, grown gross,
    Penrod—were it the stare of home-town homes'
    Shenanigans in knickers? sniggering days
    With silly pranks, and punishments that whined
    Like drowning puppies—Though later you didn't mind? . . .

    For always some shyer one stood at bay
    Pigeon-toed, bashful, that would force its way
    On summer evenings, in the stuffed settee:
    Then *Marj'rie be my fair and faithful love*
    Trilled hotly through the darkness; no one there
    But an echo, maybe; the demon with frightened hair
    Fading before you as you climbed the stair
    Left you with sister, or the bug-like whine of mother;

While you found your hangout in the backyard barn
A subtle rebellion from your God, and father;
Were the Fair Prince or the harebrained scout
When legend claimed you in the familiar cap
Of Daniel Boone, the steady hero . . . Zip!
And one more redskin had been given a slip.

Till in the heartiness of affluent age
You patronize the boy you were, and yet
Your childhood teases you like a gnat; will not
Be petted, patronized, or filed away—
For memory, only, lingers a while; and Sam,
A failure in insurance, sank from town
Ages ago; once wrote to you from Maine
That all was lost, don't wish him back again.

So what can you wait for, Penrod? war closing down
On the seven handy exits from your town
Cancels the future, while the past without substance
Whines like a gentle puppy at your door . . .
Admit it at once; pet it softly and then
Stifle it, as you have to, till it's gone
In a spreading darkness deeper than Boone's own
Hearty oblivion (a world beyond despair)
Till you grow up, full man at last—or die,
Staunch mummy, heart-shrivelled in the wind of time.

CANTICLE 1

When love invades the suburbs with an odor of oils,
Celery savors and the fragrance of soap in cellars,
With streamers of saffron locked in the little homes;

When love invades, astonishingly down
On stucco-colored bungalows, and soon
Diffuses like a wave his spreading warmth;

And the artilleries of love triumphal
On parks, on clothes-lines, on the uncertain trees,
Burst flowering out like a strangely beautiful flak;

Then housewives shake their chains, cats roll in sleep,
Pajamaed husbands, startledly waking, see
The flares of love, his gunflash crowning hills;

And even clocks turn traitor: invidious spoons
Devise an end of servitude; they sprint
Like terriers off to the ponds and vigor of March!

Dailies unfold and read themselves: the chairs
Infuriatingly berserk, circle the room
Sobbing Hosannas while climbing the stairs . . .

And what rapes upon their wills, those ones who are
    conquered!
And how sullenly they will bear the great tyrant's yoke
Who clanks through boulevards his damaging pomp,

Causing soft terror when the winged battalions
Shear down old timbers and the house of time—
And ruin everything in the name of Love.

NIGHT LETTER

I

When men abandon hands, and sail away
In sleep on beds, in streets upon a town,
It is the curvure of their motionless journey,
Spending them outwards, gives voyage to the soul;

But leaves them sleeping, lost in the dark, who seem
Delicate freightage on the night-bound feathers,
Tossed silken hair awry; spilled wrist and ankle
On muslin rafts and tided they know not whither;

II

Till the body known by daylight bestial,
Gross and ungracious, in night's filter is
Reckless in transit from its passive day.
Now young, industrious masters of dark spray,

Their limbs in jackets like developing seeds
Steep in their sea-beds, spiralling like lines
That swaying masts print in imagined air—
Tangential, maybe, to some quieter star.

III

So some, the fortunate, may believe they voyage
On a summer's cruise and runaway from day,
That ocean a plucky pond where, blithe as yachts,
Their long keels bevel the insouciant waves.

All crests now thunder under them; they move
Delightfully sundered from hatred or love,
Serene as stones; and sprawl on sunny decks
Through docile seas plegmatic as old heirlooms.

IV

But others more sadly, more obscurely voyage
On arctic oceans through gnashing squalls
Where sleet skips to the water and Ships of Doom
Deliver them to a terror's forfeit image:

The screeching dream and the hag-ridden nightmare
That all wake up to when they wake and moan
In hot pajamas freezing with chilly sweat,
This still submerging night

V

That extends so evenly, and that offers them
Its placid semblance roiled about with stars,
With milky, moon-fresh meetings, or the salt
Quick ache of parting in the muffled dark;

Till they sail at last on sufferance of their watches
(Through divisions of the darkness, and the dawn
Hissing like lava down the eastern hills,
Comber still mounting comber like a range)—

VI

Whose adventures never end with ending night:
But another sea replaces, and the dark remains;
And quiet as criminals, men who will work
Re-employ patience in their dawn-white rooms.

Somewhere a car sits idling in the darkness,
Somewhere a tiring hound spits out late whining—
Somewhere a kitten in the hazy sun
Screams its hot look of lava, and lies still.

VII

Streets rise up hissing with the tread of traffick—
Sharp firing of a motor like a gun:
And, like a gun, the license of this dawn
Where sunlight lingers, puffy as a face,

In quick delays on the spent beginnings of effort
Now transpiring in everyone's rented room,
Who now assumes—as others put away—
The endless resurrections of each day.

THE FOOTPRINT

This moonlight lying on the sand like frost,
Still with the hums of autumn, still with its old
Attendant sleepy air, limns in the lost
Poplars beside the river's bank . . . The cold
Sand is not earthly; nor anything I've known,
Familiar though it is in this easy light,
Can reassure my wandering tonight;
Yet here is one who walks—and is alone . . .

So I have cause, if any upright thing
Waits to be done, to do it now, for here
This crystal light suggests good cause to fear
My own, or others' motives; with a print,
Filling with water in the sand, to hint
How someone else stood frightened here to feel
The promptings of the moonlight in this place:

I know the name, but have forgot the face,
Whether killed or killer; the arresting stranger
Or adolescent in his drive to danger
That sent him as a fugitive through the park;
But if in madness, or a schoolboy's lark,
His shame is lost as deeply as the answer
He must have been seeking, and that brought him here.

Now what stray impulse, what maddening swoon,
Sent him like me to mark the hazy moon
And feel these rootless promptings of new shame,
Till he forgot his heritage and name,
Must stay a puzzle;—for I run quickly home,
Relieved for the light that meets me at the gate
And a soft voice grumbling, "Hurry to bed. It is late."

POEM WRITTEN IN LATE AUTUMN

There grows a strictness to some winter days
(My wildest season, as it is the wind's);
Landscapes hold distance whose horizons rise
To trouble childhood as the air's unkind—
Blow, winter winds, to equal my own mind.

And children rush to action: with their sleds
Twisting through sleet, they hitch themselves behind
Fast-racing cars, or congregate by sheds
Where warring snowballs scatter from fast hands—
(*Blow, winter winds, to equal my own mind*).

I too, a child, have mustered in those wars,
Life's freezing classroom, till a brawling friend
Threw out a snowball that assailed my eyes:
I came along love's landscape, almost blind—
(*Blow, winter winds, to equal my own mind*).

What telescoping years now huddle between
I cannot hope to hope. The airs unkind
Of wars that swept my friends off crack my brow.
That schoolyard freezes; truly its wars are blind . . .
(*Blow, winter winds, to equal my own mind*).

ENVOY

While it's a landscape only the mind can love
That brings us to such recent wars, where fear's
A natural language, and the starving dove
Of peace by huger bombs is driven blind,
Blow, winter winds, to equal my own mind.

A CLASSIC TALE

"Circe, I'll see to you!"
So did the haunted traveller say
Who gave a sad wave on the bay—
"Till moons are red and deaths are blue
(Which won't be long, as times may prove)
I give you, Queen, my total love."

But later, passing the enviable islands,
Outlasting the tedious come-ons of the sirens
To pour within the furrows of the grave
That steaming blood, he found in each close shave
A matter for more fresh forgetfulness—

Till, in some pause that waited on distress,
Things might return: dark perfumes and a dress
To daze his senses; limbs both long and fair,
And kisses that would wildly curl his hair.

And if later he told to all the common street
How Circe's no less common love was sweet,
And if in barracks, with his swinish corps,
He bragged the conquest of a goddess-whore,
The ache, the pang of longing, were still there,
Though sullied so; till he retired, forlorn,
Cursing his weakness in a flood of scorn:
"I am, I think, five total kinds of fool
To slight this lenient goddess out of school;
What if her curses shrivelled me like fire?
Could I atone for what is still desire
Probing my heart?—How thick the arrows come
To fork me with my misery and shame!"

Until, forgiving all, she knelt to him
Out of the puzzling darkness of a dream
Soothing and healing; till, being undone, he cried
"The bliss, O Queen, of sleeping at your side,
Not once till now denied
Till I, a mortal, thus zanily presumed—
Stays with me now, till I am all consumed.

"Did I dream those arms, in the night by the bay?
Indeed, great Queen, I cannot dream them away
But curse myself, that I have changed for them
A world of sights, where all's confused and dim,
Your pastoral simplicities
Exchanging for these dark intricacies."

She would have calmed, sad mist, with lying words
His head that puzzled amid mocking birds,
Perplexed by travelling; but he cut short
Her efforts with a final, meant retort:

"Let me die, Virgin, if I remember thee;
But let me die virgin, if I forget thee,"

That faded along the sea-wall . . . Night was spent;
He lumbered like a lubber to his tent;
This night and its events had left him flat . . .
The next day he got drunk again; and that was that.

THE WANDERER UPON SUNSETS

Above the marshland, in the western sky,
Now, with the sun descending, half of light
Crumples away, the rest more radiantly
Tinging through trees the water. Now the night
Waits calmly for the balanced end of day,
As herons hover, poising in just-soft flight.

The transient will, once overmastered, there
Fell thankfully into its world of peace
And tremorless quiet: and the settled air
Resolved that likeness of a wilderness
To a fresh and lucid beautiful. Elsewhere,
It seemed, existed darker wilderness,

A bitter land, too hard at last to tame,
Where nothing lived for man to live upon,
Who lurched unbalanced through the withering flame
Of suns below the equinoctial line,
And sank himself in an unending shame.
Yet how peacefully *this* sunset settles in!

Poising within our cloud-massed western sky
The heron waits on silence, and the night
Offers Valhallas for the shaping eye
That sees in far peninsulas of light
(Gleaming against the dark, like jewels, brightly)
A lucid order to perpetuate;

Still to be found a fugitive romancer
Proposing endless sunset, as a man
Stands heron to the night—or as a dancer,
In easy equipoise advancing on
To shameful death, that is his balanced answer,
Pivots as softly as this setting sun.

WRITTEN IN DEJECTION

"Remote, unfriended, melancholy, slow"
Sad rain converges on the tin
Roof of the quonset I am sheltered in
With sixty other men or so;

Who talk, or gripe at cards. The surge
Of noise recedes like gentle rain;
Rising, it re-ebbs again . . .
Till I am moved by a vast urge

Voiceless as sorrow to be quits with this
Relentless world of tide and talk;
Traitorous, I would stalk
Some vaster emptiness, where it lies.

There brainless plants with sighing heads
Fringe the dim air. Laconic moans
Are wistful in their monotones
Of nothing meant and less said:

Dim valves, soft tunnels: the minds of beasts
Maundering through the thickset air
Must be our modernest despair:
A howling vacuum sobbing through life.

And so I calculate this hut
Of noise to be the common stage
Of perfect nothing, by which our age
Is speeding towards—no matter what!

NOTE VERGING ON SWANSONG

When the falconer shall clamp a hated hood
Upon my head; or the silly spectre calls
Out of the silly past, intent on blood,
My blood, and the nodding terror falls
Till "I come, Albert Herzing, I come for YOU,"

A voice resounds throughout the ringing skies—
Then I am ready, Lord, to treat of Thee,
With many metaphors and images
Serving the turn: compare it to the sea
Saying "I come, Albert Herzing, I come for YOU,"

As walking by the margin of the main
And buoyant ocean, some busy wave awaking,
Enraged at my infinity, complains:
"Now therefore do I send my breakers breaking
And come, Albert Herzing, and come for YOU";

Indefatigably, when I am darting
Across a busy street, late afternoon
Lost among horns, some carburetor's spitting,
As windswept out of silence, softly intones
"I come, Albert Herzing, I come for YOU,"—

Thus till the falconer dissevers me
From the blinding hood, and I am set to wing
Through finite pastures in the upper sky,
To realms of God, where even angels sing,
"Welcome, Albert Herzing, we welcome *YOU.*"

BOWERY IN WINTER

I

These random, sad, unsteady men, who leap
Like madmen out of the cop-hot dark,
Ranging like toms through the windy park,
Group late at night by wood-fires in a heap,
Blue-skinned and trembling, where the pad-foot snow's
An aimless cover-up that rapidly flows
In gusts and eddies through the quiet night—
And flows all night: the infernal chill of the light
That whirls above them; concussive stars
That pin-point in the eyes like moons,
Dangerous wars, and rockets, crowd to the eye,
Stirred by an alcohol that makes them spin
In rigid circles, till they quietly die
With sirens, taxis, and adrenalin.

II

Then here where sorrow, an agonizing sorrow
Has swept them low, and undermines the nails
Of their crazy fingers, or creeps upon the hair
Like a fear (once maybe one from love
Took bitter draughts; or maybe a late scholar
From leafing over books went daffy and drank
His way past all position, till he sank
To this lowest of all: this grim place, where a dollar
Is cursingly mocked at and rules everything)—
Here in the depths, where wretchedness is king
Of life, I hear the ghost of Bodenheim crying
"Protect us, Mary, in the steady dying
We lend our lives to!" and his far-off cry:
"Save us, O Lord, from dying!—now that we die."

THE MOTHER OF THE AMAZONS

Imperious, maternal, tall,
The mother of the mothers of us all
Rests everywhere . . . Granitic under the earth
In strata, or lost among white clouds
Over the mountains; mirrored in rivers wherever
The willows bend to cover her, she is
Unsearchable in all her mysteries,
Unreachable by human sense
Beautiful, timeless, and immense.

If in her daughters she reposes,
Fair goddesses whose many forms
Permeate the earth in swarms—
Ceres, Maya, Mother Mary—
Our first warm thoughts, our latest cries
Involve her; are to her
An anguished tribute, wholly dear.

As we are dear to her,
As she herself is dear,
Each leans to her in prayer,

"Great Mother, bend to, heal
This dying child."

THE EARTHWORM

When the night had spent its gentle weight of rain
And day came early, its yellow on the trees
Prompting precocious song in the hearts of birds,
There broke from damp coverts a tunnel-dark earthworm
With mute clamberings to attain the pavement:
And his silver track seemed such a soft wake
That I thought how soon some narrowing beak
Must rush to drill him downwards, till to his death
He fumbles the hemmed-in substance of his breath . . .

But the noon's sun cast contrary dice:
Side-glancing heat, the stroke at the bone,
Pushing hot advantage, quickly surprised
His ambushed heart in the center of all its anguish—
Moved inwards on him, till of that little beast
There quickly sizzled such a sunburnt paste
That not one robin, brawny-sinewed lord
Of a whirring country, with wings and whistles
Would fly to sink for, or find good to the taste . . .

But the honey-bee made a ravishing moan
In the luscious forage of his life, and the wind
Left me to celebrate in that savage scene
Life-wishing things; all those that creep and crawl,
Fly, scuttle, clamber, or sit perfectly still—
The toad that hops from his dusty cupboard
Into broad sunshine, and is quickly clobbered
By squealing urchins; or always another
Stabbed by a brother or moaning for a mother;

Sweet others like earthworms, who are known by a flip-flop
So madly adventurous that they often hop
Off beaten paths and get a laugh— Though death
Is lunging about their pavements, and will sheathe
Far-ranging pincers where the flyaway heart
Spurts scarifyingly, flips over wildly, and goes
A meagre journey to its gaunt repose
Far away and dark—till Christ and Kingdom Come
And the dyings of earthworms motion the way from the tomb:

With badgers arising in robes of resurrection,
And His small creatures spiralling up towards God.

THE NEEDLE'S GRIEF

    The needle weeps for wounds
    That still must flex a stitch—

    (It must have sensed a scar
    Perched in itself somewhere
    Incalculably far
    Through muted wards of time
    To suffer so, or else have winced
    At the curing of a prince,
    While kingdoms locked and swayed,
    That now it rushes in silence
    Its healing trade)—
                     and weeps for wars,
    Blood, diseases, and certain scars—
    Far beyond our time and tears
    It works its way across
    Man's badgering loss,
    Till time is sinewed and embossed
    With hems—each stitch a seeping bead
    On rosaries of human blood.

    (The starlight must have heard it howl:
    The starlight must have heard us howl.

    The blood swells in its chafered bowl.)

    And the needle, stitching onwards, weeps for wounds.

DIRGE

My uncle roared and buckled like a goat
That day he took a sea-bass by the throat
And flensed it with a knife. (It made the cry
That dumb creation makes before it dies

Like a cat's childish mewl, and yet almost
As if there were a tender, speechless ghost
That cried for love and understanding in
The spirit, pinioned between gill and fin).

My uncle's spirit battered at those bars
Like dumb things also, swarming up the roars
Of foam to breed—till it fell back against
A rock that landed him on circumstance

And left him vanquished; neither by the verge
Of savage shores where sea-bass, in an urge
To try themselves by slaughter, crowd around
The angler's bait; nor in the twilight sound

Of fading sea-birds will you watch him stand
And flail at fish that still evade his hand
Till with a vicious lug he pulls them in;
For twilight sees my furious uncle gone

Now from those vigils, and white walls hold him close—
His dreaming visage, sombre and morose,
Seems to see wildly, flashing in the flood,
Huge fishes thrashing landwards, flecked with blood.

ODE: ON A DISTANT PROSPECT OF KENYON COLLEGE

Sun-mellowing halls, that pin the sky—
The blandishments of learning lie
Along your greying columns, high
On breezeless days how breathless, and seem
How still, as in some quieter dream:

Summer meandering through the cool
Sunlight, like a foreign pool
Burnished to seem the untaught school
Of tatterdemalion images
By which the random heart most lives—

Till at last they're drawn in the whole scene:
A searching atmosphere, serene
By distances through which we scan
The further hills; the conscious way
That sees a furtive holiday

Extending placidly through time—
A velvet-soft continuum
That flows remotely through the dim
Hours of existence that we know
When friends and laughter let our bodies go!

So contemplation marks the hill
With solitude, and still
Man's purpose cannot nudge the will
To action yet, and I am bound
Fast in a daily, studious round,

Swept inwards in the dizzying drain
Of time, that sends a bumptious train
Or bark of country dogs to align
The mind with memory and peg the hill
With hazes, glad and beautiful.

And so, goodbye; I say goodbye
Because I obviously can't stay—
Trains scoot me homewards, and will hoot me over
The world—yet looking back
I find how thin and narrow is the track
That holds me off . . . Take then, dear lovely place,
The gratitude of this, your latest lover.

THE BOWERY

Hierarchies even among the poor
Can be observed; and here, in sorrow's corner,
They stand, lie, lurch at every street and door
Like dying spastics—till if a bum has been
Winsome as blazes or deformed as sin
No longer matters: his life-light, clumsily smeared
In the backs of ledgers, is soon cashiered
To the sad accompaniment of the withering rain.

Till then, befriend him; seek his world, and he
Might suddenly swivel on you with a key,
A gaunt man with a towering sorrow
To sponsor you through his Inferno
Like a dread Virgil, instructing where they go
Who are shifted about as the winds blow:
Fogs of Avernus; stale sleets, and fiery rains,
Will thank the kindly traveller for his pains . . .

And yet, his hell once entered, and its queer
Eternal sufferers once listened to,
Sympathised with, or guided to a beer
That won't allay their savage thirst, may you
Emerge with pathos to the upper air
That stabs your lungs: Park, Lexington, and Fifth,
A short trek homeward, dozing through the drift
Of human souls that pass like whirling snow
Before your eyes; and you've nowhere to go—
Nowhere on the damned earth now.

THE STUDENTS

The slow-paced ones, who labor to be certain,
Raise around their teacher a curtain
Of careful days, of grammar-drill and chalk
That cloisters up his life again, until
His seems a world of too-recurrent talk
Where words are valueless—for they,
The valued currency
He wore his life out to amass, become
With repetition numb
And fading like inscriptions on a tomb
That threatens to engulf him, words and all
Fibbing of the life within
Growing so thin
And listless that it will not hide a grave
Repining thought that his indeed is one
Of those sad lives whose profit is uncertain
Who work, but hope no gain
Who harvest pains.

Or so it seems.
So, in dark nights, when evaluation
Beats like a vein in his relentless head
Until he screams, "I didn't mean to mean
Whatever I seemed to mean—although I meant it!"
And, crying like a man demented,
He wakes outside the chores of sleep
Into a deep
And final funk, at which the students say
"Mr. Herzing's just himself today!"

So will his life relentlessly become
Untenably like a tomb
In which he hears the distant drum
Of mourners going away,
Going to stay
In their own world of life

Unless a ray
Scatters within, and a youth's bright eye
Comes clear with thought, as he says thoughtfully
"Oh yes. I see. I see!"

WHAT THE CORMORANT SANG

"Let the hawks circle in air as blue as powder
And of such radiance and such peaceable blue
That the hum of crickets, spell of bees is louder
Than cannon is, or mortar . . . Let soft shade
Be hushed with awful quietude, for man
Nor is in love nor happy to be loved—"

So sang the cormorant, and swiftly ran
Through the blue, voluble air, above the shaved
And splintered landscape of the testing ground.
Summer it was. Silence and sullen heat
Rose from the proving-guns in coils that bound
Their steaming tresses along the desert's rock—

Soft insect voices chorused; other sounds
Were numb, except gay warfare's whispering din,
To counterpoint that cormorant's sweet song,
While tanks most pointedly impaled the dun
And heaving desert where an enemy
Lurked and feared behind each half-hid dune . . .

Was it Cassandra through that desert air?
Vague shape of prophecy; the courier
Of stunned eternity? Agamemnon dead,
Rancor and blood distained his dusty head . . .
The cormorant sees horizons and moving on
Hums requiem for the passing time of man.

RESPONSIBILITY

And the strikes come, and in the drying hills,
Where angry dawn its busy rancor spills
On cougars and on quonsets, glib men plan
Swift forays to the hinterlands of Hell
And the heart of fever. Massacred to the man!

So Heaven's intolerance descends on one
Who falls and fails, jerking upright again
To fall and fail again on peakèd rocks
Slanted like tables towards the surgical sun—
At length being patient whom distemper shakes,

Still unresigned, undisciplined to endure,
Not curable suffers his detested cure:
Outrageously aloof in deadly languor
He dies on tablelands whose shards conspire
Like leeches, and sap him from his root of anger.

—So might the Wanderer snarl, turn heart away,
And, holding gentlest nose, ascend the sky
Like a film run backwards. The tableland remains.
Awareness, like a slow disease, remains.
Inverted, the film displays a truer scene:
The responsibility of being born man!

THE SPENT SUBSTANCE

I

Rimbaud wrote a book and suffered to write it,
Paced quickly in his room like something pent,
Time pacing out—and when nobody read it,
He burst his cage, this hated Occident,
And plundered Abyssinia from a tent.

While Emerson, who taught the Over-soul,
Anemic udder to an earth of forms,
Died painlessly in bed, and on the whole
Was right at heart: though born infirm
He fought through sickness to achieve his soul,

And truly lost the world's—leaving a scar
We cannot think of till we flex the stitch
He zippered down the globe: a bleeding suture
Emitting a pus of terror that we scratch,
Patch up and anguish, but leading to no future.

And Kurtz, in hungry Africa, can tell
How the trees thickened and their shadows massed:
There too, there too, the days had a dark smell:
They stank of duty as they feebly passed—
And that was how he knew he was in hell.

II

Pale horse, and paling rider, Pegasus
Mounts with a vocal burden . . . When it falls
Its death-song down the air is amorous
As day's last crumpling over waterfalls
Mourned by the poet—loved by Orpheus

Who took a second look at death, and lived
Thereafter with his grief and loss—like these,
Incurably Romantic! and like us
(Though greater were his skill and art)
Torn by the furies of his sad, ambivalent heart.

ELEGY FOR A SUICIDE

I

All suffering was pointless: soon or late
Anguish and Africa would require his guns
To spray with ruthlessness a furious fate.

Butchered, battered, he'd wrangle in anyone's wars
For simple fame—not fortune, lest his days
Bonanzas might be to usurers and whores.

Even death was pointless then: his enemies
Wildly would smack his conquered body down,
Worms snarl in the dustproof hollows of his eyes.

—Which knowledge goaded; oh it quietly perplexed
His shrewder dealings in that simple game,
Knowing the cards to be marked, and the dice "fixed"

By prancing sharpers who had sworn an oath
That one more euchre and they'd have him whole—
Till, tossing in his hand, he dealt out death.

Then shy, eccentric, meticulous as before,
Wearing his slicker, always the poker face!
He shuffled off precisely towards what star.

II

Great griefs are silent: therefore let
Me be his voice in all his grieving
Who, shrieking, turning and twisting, shot
Down forty full floors to the perilous paving.

Whom forty floors the curtains waved
From gasping windows fast farewell:
Who died because he never lived:
Lifeless, he absconds to Hell

Leaving us but a mound above.
Trapped in which little room he screams
And beats against the wall and shoves
The lid away. Or perhaps he dreams? . . .

Great griefs are silent: therefore let
Me be his voice in all his grieving
Who, shrieking, turning and twisting, shot
Down forty full floors to the perilous paving.

III

All suffering is pointless: soon or late
All silent griefs must spring to speaking acts.
Faced by their sorrow, badgered by needling cops,

Deserted promptly by their summer friends
To the pitfalls of a massive Pity,
They move about to hurly-burly ends:

As when the images of death parade
In the brief desert of a darkened room,
One's fascinating grimaces recede—

In a dearth of words he is carried home
Where piece-meal all shall follow him.
Friend, in the portals where you are,
Wait thou by Cerberus—we shall meet thee there!

BALLADE FOR DYING LADIES

Goodbye sweet Stupid Lil and Happy Bea;
Goodbye, Miss Whortle! And, Miss Chapp, goodbye!
And Fay who was a wise one (*Goodbye, Fay!*)—
And to Bunny the roarer, and to Sleepy Lou,
And to Mrs. Blurp who suddenly had to go,
And to sloppy Fran, and Meg: Goodbye! Goodbye!

(Death deals so harshly with a Lady's frame,
You'd think he'd learn more chivalry—though, true,
He opens a Door for her and lets her through;
But will not take the curb to her; is slow
To recognize her justifiable claim
That he be Knight, and tender; proves untrue

With his frivolous kisses; polygamist!
He cares not whether she's kissed or unkissed
But like Bluebeard, he no sooner chops one up
Than another one is taken in to sup;
An adulterer, he steals his way to homes
Not his; no girl knows when he comes

Lying scared Danae to that clasp of death
And he will take her and will stop her breath
And lay her down and close her in and shut
The door forever . . . No use raising a shout:
He has come for many, he will come for you:
Goodbye, Fran! Goodbye, Peg! Goodbye, Lou!)

THE BLESSING

        This perfect green has held
        Hesperidean wine
        Lighter but no clearer
        Than its image in a mirror
        Or pools of fragrance to the taste;
        Prouder than a vase
        But humbler than an urn,
        It must have served its turn
        Admirably to grace
        An emperor's banquet, but—
        Such being the times—its spout
        Has poured for me alone
        This lightly perfect wine.

FRAGONARD

Being so elegantly
Restrained by Art, not Nature,
A lovely creature
Swings up high
So lightly free
That we are rendered dizzy
Watching her easy
Ascension up the slopes,
The painted slopes of air,
With white hands on the ropes
And heels kicked high
Above the tops
Of the shivering trees.

Desire the more obvious
For being unambitious,
A gallant of the time
Stares upon her knees
While everything he sees
Clearly pleases him:
He leans back in the shrubbery
With knees gone slightly rubbery,
Seared mightily with all the fire
Of an immaculate desire.

How well their painter knew
The heart of graceful actions,
Everything fluidly
Moving in line
To form a total One,
A painting without fractions
That left them frozen here forever,
Moving and lovely and frozen forever.

THE STATUE AND THE PARK

Simon Bolivar, who holds on top his head
A pigeon, stares with the wild blind eyes
Of the stone he is, and stares uncomforted,
Five thousand miles from Quito and
Old revolutions . . . On his either hand
Welter those rushed participants of life,
The people: a multitude that paces
Heavy with parcels and the driven faces
And tight-held heads commanded by precision:
Only the sun in mellowing derision
Hoots at them mercilessly, till they see as a child
Their world new-fashioned, dazzling bright and wild . . .

Yet children, very active, drift at play
In proctored squadrons—aimlessly trotting
With wobbly steps, they prattle and run round
This great green play-pen that their parents found
Before them—and nothing of it seems wild;
Nothing of it is night or revolt or the weather
Of dreams; and the statue's eyes are rotting
In a pock-marked, stained endurance of what they see:
The trees, the buildings, the children, the day
Through fractured vision must have gone astray
To sink in emptiness as useless as
The dust that filters day-long through the grass . . .

Yet have the wind rise up, have it touch lightly
The quicksilver leaves: there quickens so much grace,
Almost it's uncontrollable; almost it pours
Beyond the boundary of these waltzing acres;
Trees quiver their dust off, and children roar
Like mad things at their frantic play.
Green errands cataracting into day
Crowd from a source of amplitude; each creature
In a lucky instant makes speedy headway,
Till the statue sees—come in its timeless nature
To order all this ravished scene—
A splendid, savage hour, gone wild with green.

THE REVOLT OF THE CHILD

A spin, a hardy spin—and here's the globe
In the schoolroom reeling; seas and countries,
Purples and greens, and pinks and azures, fly
On the dizzy axis of futurity—
While with candid, captious attitudes, the curled
And lounging students fix a half-bored eye
Upon their teacher, and otherwise prefer
Dark dreams of football to her history,
And broils a schoolroom off—while one, whose eyes
With swift evasion slide in a small, wild face,
Hair scribbled about in tangled snarls of lace,
Veers to a future none of them may know.

There where the darkness and the undertow
By Africa and the cliffs of Teneriffe
Reel with the stars; where tart, alluvial spray
And sea-salt darken his rebellious way,
He travels to an unknown ocean—gone
Into a world that's calmer and more alone
Than any schoolroom, until he's far away
From where his friends, with desks and crayons, lie
Tumbled at the bottom of a sea
Beyond him still, and gratefully beyond
His attitudes, now gathering as his mind
Deploys in oceans cooler and more kind.

—"Here's where *we* are!" the teacher snaps. He nods;
Of course she is not right; and he is not here,
Though companions all surround him in warm crowds
With snickers, braids and spitballs, and the clear
Flute-like, piping voices of the still unsure—
Till the schoolroom fades, its teacher fades; the sea
Slips in its foam, skids to oblivion
Her world, the future:

And he is lost in oceans while he thinks
"They'll never find me here"—and he is right;
Neither the sea-bird nor the bird-ringed liner,
Nor Crusoe's raft, nor any imploring gesture
Of thoughtful love, shall ever find him here.

FIRES OF HOME: POEMS

By JOHN M. RIDLAND

Copyright © 1961 John M. Ridland

For Muriel

ELEGY BY THE YOUNGER BROTHER
(for R.F.R. and J.G.R.)

1. I hurry down the wound roads of Scotland
to answer my Father, urgent on the phone,
through green hangings and yellow glens to bring
these first flowers of your final Spring,
Snowdrops I picked, waiting for the bus.

2. I reach the house and find you have hung on—
my coming only gave you this day of living.
But now the Snowdrops steal the oxygen
from your deep breathing.

3. Too late for you to smell, to more than see,
they must not breathe or you relapse,
these fatal flowers of your last Spring.
And yet they do, and you sleep into Death.

4. Your final beauty blooms for us
within the pallor of your lying dead.
The last tears of my childhood are shed.
Strangely, in your death, there is this exultation.

5. My Father and my older brother,
being grown into the world and life
which I step barely over the threshold of,
gave you their greater love—
and yet my love is perfect, knowing no other,
more fully and more blindly yours.

6. My brother's voice shakes with his tears.
The clay he's man of quakes with this passion;
it carries through the wires across an ocean
and fills the air that fills my ear with grief.
Your lost daughters' youth dies in your eyes.
O brother, in unbelief accept thou my belief!

7   My hand takes paint, and in the shapes of brown
    portrays bereavement, which my mind
    cannot form: neither can my tongue speak.
    The strong spirit weeps but the flesh is weak.
    It is your flesh only I can inherit.
    What lies here dead, is your erect spirit.

8   Unkindly you die as life begins in me
    to make me man.
    A boy only I picked this flower
    which strikes the final second of your hour.
    *Never, at your lost daughters' wedding, would you have been
        more alive.*

SONS OF CAIN

(In the middle ages, the artist was sometimes considered a descendant of Cain, and thus tainted with Cain's guilt.)

    And as if it were no more than a shock of hay
    Or of full corn lopped by a steady reaper,
    And as if he would feel no more guilt than that of a bird
    For the crushing of grubs when the stalk breaks and topples,
    And as if in the sunlight the white glint, the gleam,
    The sweep in an arc up and above and over
    And down,
    In the hot day with a fine dust rising behind
    And ripples glazing the flat road to Damascus—
    While the women at home and his hoary father sit
    In the thick shade under great mud walls
    Swallowing cool wine from half-scooped gourds
    By the low rough table, while their tall dark sister,
    Her jug on her head balanced, with one arm raised
    And her breast firm that even he had eyed,
    Swayingly walked to the well and filled the pitcher
    Scanning the dusty road to the fields
    And then turned homeward, placing the jug in the shade—
    While all the time like a wild bird swooping to clip
    The firm stalk under its ripe head,
    In a flash of noontime sun on the dust-lined
    Shining metal, the sickle fell with a dead sound.
    And again fell. And again.

    And Cain looked up with fear as a dry wind
    Rustled the olives there at the hill's rim
    And he in the lee of the hill hidden and tearless
    Alone with the hanging scythe and what he had done.
    While on the warm breeze from a sudden lake (a jewel
    Among dry hills) swept the smell of olives
    And red wine and cakes baking and ever
    The smell of a woman beside him lying
    On the cool rushes on the damp green rushes

Of an inner room and the woman part of the room
And part of the smell of olives, and all of them
Part of all he would never again know.

But the dust then whirled the cool smell out of his nostrils
And even the olive trees looked brown in the sun
With the ground below him red and the curving thing
In his hand still, and the sweat still on his neck
That the wind would not dry,
And ahead of him nothing but dust in the rising road
And a forever of reaping, an eternal raising
The smooth scythe, an endless swinging it down,
And making or carving something from what was there,
From what lay red and still in the road ahead.
But always Abel his brother is dead, lies dead at his feet
With his throat and neck red from his own blood
While evermore
The one tall sister and his many cousins
And his white-bearded father wait in the cool house,
Drinking the wine he will never taste again.

1951

SIERRA: SEPTEMBER 1959

In every country I have gone to, there have been truth-tellers and
    liars,
indistinguishable in clothing, speech, gestures,
except for the turn of their eyes. Nowhere
more than here in these mountains.
                                      Nothing was ever
more truthful than these lodgepole pines, these two in particular,
posing in their upper sections to be monuments to this moment.

Or monuments to the lost Jews and children of Warsaw, when
    twenty years
ago, . . . the drums of destruction
hurried towards them as the lies of Hitler ripened.
They held themselves together as sparsely as possible,
growing small needles for the small rain like these pines.

And pointed straight upwards to withstand the slant of bombs heavy
    as snowfall:
their 20-year straightness behind them as they prepare to go down
in the silence in which trees fall, it is said, in the silent forest.

HERE'S THE STEEPLE

(Variation on the childhood game)

        The spired rocket perches on its one
        but many-footed firm foundation
        beside a beach in Florida;
        and men of science kneel to their orisons
        of *kyrie* and *gloria* before
        instrumental altars in their chapels.

        Now here's our variation:
        it's religion brings us to be watchers;
        it's we, who are not Pilates, are the
        crowd. Now when the countdown finishes
        one reaches zero. That is to say,
        the spire of *our* cathedral
        neither crumbles nor falls
        but with a crucified roar
        ambles godward and *is* of a sudden
        while our necks jolt back in awe
        church city Christ Caesar and all.

        Open the doors and see all the people.

LAMENT FOR THE DEAD TEN THOUSANDS

(The major who led the first atomic attack, under examination by psychiatrists, told reporters: "I do feel I killed those people at Hiroshima.")

We saw it in technicolor—you may not,
But must believe, from the documentary shots,
That day was black-and-white as the black deed
And the white dying and the mushroom cloud.

The white crying of the souls aloud
Splattered our under-fuselage with their flak—
The sky-pale belly under the sea-dark back—
On their heavenward journey through their death and prayer
From the total blinded whiteness of their pyre:
Their psalming more than shrapnel struck my head.
    O, I was the finger and thumb
    Pinched the trigger and loosed the bomb,
    The chained dog of disaster
    Slipped by his well-trained master.

And homeward on our wings we dragged the dead
Ten thousands, ten ten thousands in their bloody
Or bloodless intake of their final pain,
Exhaled in vapors on my wings to stain
The bright aluminum purpose in my brain.

To foil the swift completion of my mission,
The one atom whose giant fission
Exploded into dense Japan
Was the equilibrium of Man.
    O, I was the dummy Adam
    Pinched the apple and loosed the bomb.

I have kept no track of my crew—
Whether they, in every August, too,
Dodge the high artillery of guilt,
Cleaving the clouds of death our action built
Sky-high, fogging the sunlight of the day;
Or did remembrance in them rust away?

I have not plugged the holes in my gas tank yet,
Nor can I cross my log out and forget
One hundred thousand died, wherever they hid—
I FEEL I KILLED THEM; AND I DID:
    I was the finger and thumb
    Pinched the trigger and loosed the bomb.

In summer-rain on relieved city or hill
The fall-out of our Fall is falling still.
    O, I was the finger and thumb
    Pinched the trigger and loosed the bomb,
    I was the dummy-master
    Slipped the dogs of all disaster.

POLITICAL POEM 1960

(*After reading Yeats's "Easter 1916"*)

        Ah Yeats! you turn me to myself
        again, & away from myself.
        Petrifactions of the obsessed
        intellect—angers
        of the enchancred heart—
        the huge terrors of political thought:
        over them all, the shadow
        of the living sun, the purl
        of the stream alive, plash
        of horse-hoof, pass,
        rustle of chaparral
        behind the disappearing
        bobtailed cottontail,
        hasty crackle
        and close of brush
        on the invisible deer.

                *

        Out of sight on the
        invisible plateaus
        of blank air,
        where the U-2's
        chase the arching missiles,
        under the tin tops
        of Khrushchev and Eisenhower
        & the world's press,
        a mother's soft intercession
        rises, like a prayer in the old days
        when they thought a God—

some old codger
looking after things—
inhabited that crackling,
humming space.

May 19, 1960

NOON BREAK
(*Lieutenant's Report*)

Lacking a foe, our soldiers fight each other.
The Jewish Negro fights the Jew.
And Jones fights Jones. I fear:
I will not step between while they are swinging,
For they mean death, I know. Last night,
Robertson the white was nearly finished
By Robertson his brother, the Negro.

We break at noon. And now,
In March, unregimented, spring
Stretches its credible idea of warmth
Over our soldiers in a trial run. The sun
Spreads through the leaves and lights the strength of one
Who wears the sheathed but lethal bayonet
Well to his side—relaxed, released
From every duty of sense, almost asleep.

In the rumpled unmilitant forest, the pacific land,
He is surprised. His form of youth
Took shape at street-corners. He lies
Under an oak which spreads its leaves to shed.

Nature has lost a child; she stands by the murky river.

We break to mend.
We rise. I line my men.
I send them on along the treacherous march.
Negro by Jew and Jones by Jones,
Robertson by Robertson, my risen
Man stands starched, his spit-shined boots
Cleared of their road-dust in a second. One band,
I send my soldiers into the treacherous March.
Nature stands in her grief by the murky river.

SOLDIER ON LEAVE

As if I were Caesar back from Gaul,
Or Antony strolling the streets of Rome,
I pass through a countryside full of fall
On roads that well might lead me home.
It is football weather, the balls are sent
Like lazy birds through the crisping air
To float like zeppelins over Kent
Or seagulls over the walls of Troy.
My lungs are filled with a flood of cold,
The world is a crystal filament.

The leaves are Romans lining the way,
And they burn in bunches, sacrificed.
They are sacrificing the harvest to me
For the summer's sake I left behind.
And how I deserve this ritual
None knows better than I myself,
Who am their picture of bitter spring,
The Trojan Horse and the Greeks within,
The return of the young, the fatal son
Come back to slaughter the innocent calf.

So cows and cattle shrill my name
And my bourgeois brother grits his teeth.
My father dumbly opens his store
To my noisy, filthy, and greedy mouth.
I am used to living with pigs and now
Clean my hands on the living sow.

The Roman leaves are ashes and smoke.
The neighbors offer up a ghost
In their memory of my innocence:
I become a figure in a mask.
They wear me like smiles on a whore's face.
I am laid in a painted vault of words.

CRIME REPORT

1. Introduction.

I heard on the radio
The criminal's details:
How he spat nails,
How he was unafraid
And should be considered armed.
I was naturally alarmed:
I thought, "If that hard knuckle
Knocks at my thin door,
I shall at once bolt out
With all speed heed allows
The door of my dangerous house,
Yelling for help as I run,
And all the cops will come;
I'll leave him there to them
In my implicated home
And see how wild he'll be!"
I thought, "He'll probably
Himself run any door out,
Into the loud hands
Of metal cuffs and bands."

"And that," I thought, "will be that.
They will lead him away to a cell
And during his dying fall
He can preimagine Hell."
And that would be vengeance flat.

But who'd be responsible?
And agent of his fate?
Who would've slammed the door
On his freedom with all hate?
And put the cord to his neck
And the trapdoor at his feet?
I! I his Cerberus,
Yapping at every head,

Tiny but serious,
I'd have led him into the dead,
When living, boisterous,
He trespassed on my deed.

2. Report.

The criminal in my castle
Would urinate in the sink,
Would slop himself a drink,
Would slouch on my comfy couch.
While I, the Goldielocks
To this suburban fox,
Would shout, "Somebody's peed in my pots,
And he's using too many watts!"
(For all the lights would be on
And the radio and shaver.)
And "he's robbing my salt of its savor!"

This expert criminal
Would leave evidence of his sojourn
Of value to the police:
His fingermarks on my glasses
Would yield to analysis
Essential criminal truths,
His urine in the drain
Be run through test upon test
Again and again and again,
And the prying eyes of sleuths
From cracks in the walls would wrest
The ten commands of crime
His patience carved therein.

3. Hypothesis.

But what if he never burnt,
Or dangled, or was shot,
But drew minor punishment
For the mischiefs he had wrought—

Or if, in twenty years,
He walked out on parole,
Or flew the coop again?
And I his little red hen?
Then from the day he departed
I'd be constantly alerted
Lest he find his way and return
To my comfortable home
And shame me out the door,
And, Goldielocks once more,
I'd shout, "Police!" in vain,
For all the policemen now
Would laugh, "We've already done
What you call on us to do,
And once done a job is through."
(As if that were ever true!)

But knowing he still would kill,
And was deadly still,
I'd take on myself the chore
Of guarding him, once more.

4. Conclusion.

All this is history.
The same is why I stand
Through storms of dust and snow
With a loud alarm in my hand.
I am saving the whole land
From treachery, and death—
I keep the State from the danger
Of such a criminal loose.

The price is, I am a stranger
To the walls of my own house.

ONE VOLUME SOILED

A hurricane swept in upon
This book. I was not there myself
To put it underneath a desk
Or on a safer shelf.
I underwent the hurricane
In a far-off place.

They closed the shutters, but the wet,
Like an assertive, clever thief,
Crept through the cracks; along the walls
It worked its way. When I came back,
The soaking it had brought about
Passed all belief.

Elsewhere I felt the hurricane.
But, less resistant than this book,
Which carries outward all its stain—
And not a thought or comma changed—
I bear the ravages within,
Without a blemish on my skin.

STATION OVERSEAS

On a scratching shortwave station
The favorite hits from home
Bewilder the mild palms
About this tropic barracks
And fill all soldiers' pulses
With memories of passion.

Fading pictures gather
Dust and lint as foreign
As every ancient stone
Within this Spanish bastion
Which we in turn inhabit,
Inmates of the tradition.

My one-heart and I, long
Ago at one sharp corner,
Said good-night and so-long
To our practices of pleasure.
We let our waving fingers
Cease their loving measure.

FOR A FRIEND AT SEA

        Oh, sands may shift, may shift!

        Here's my anchor dropped
        Scarce a mile from shore,
        Here's an anchorage
        Safe it seems and stable.

        But rocks themselves may wobble.

        Oh what remains to hold
        When the end of living rises,
        A flood of earth over sky?

        Bare anchorage and dry!

        Then there's an end to the fable,
        The anchor cable weighed,
        The iron itself be dried.

        Over a rocky land adrift—

        For sands may shift, may shift.

TRUCKER

I pull my cab around me
Like a cape or tent
The wipers keep from drowning
My water-threatened sight
The vision of people about
A puppet-show in the street
Is like hallucination
They are shrouded ghosts in grey
They are hallucinations
Lining the boulevard
Of practicality
They are dreams made hard.

Sometimes from my perch
Within, above, the world
That is, and is not, mine
I view these apparitions
As shadows on a screen
They are a filmy breed
Beyond my closing hut
With all the windows shut
They are unreal indeed
They make no noise or shout
They walk or move about
Using the heavy tread
Of Ajax or the dead.

But I the new Achilles
Fleet as gazelle or porpoise
Bounding as cloud or sea
I carry a heavy load
Effortlessly
I may haul the safety
Of a city behind my back
I may carry with me
Gold or steel or guns

Cotton or magnesium
Soap or butter. Once
I carried dynamite.

It doesn't matter to me
Whatever comes, comes
I hang myself on a wheel
I ease myself on a brake
I shift from second to low
I whistle to keep awake.

There are many of us about
Owning our separate nights
Brought to community
By loneliness of flesh.
We blink our lights in greeting.
Stopping out of the weather
We steal some fire from God.
We plan for the day ahead
Drinking coffee together:
Dawn in the empty streets
Morning under the mountains
Noon in the low desert
Sunset splitting a valley
Dusk above the ocean
Sleep at our destination.

These are the hopes we hold
But hope is necessity
For the dates are fixed in advance,
The time to arrive or leave
To sleep or wait for a time
Hurry or slow it down.
We are on schedule to thrust
Through the Divide at midnight
And if sun should silt the air
With luminous golden dust
(It could happen anywhere)
It's just a part of the job,
We see it because we must.

McNALLY

With two great hands he greeted the Sister:
She had called and he met her on the driveway,
But she wouldn't come in although he pressed her
But left leaving her greetings to Mrs. McNally.

He turns the ashes out of the burning-can
Waters the roses with them;
And there are other plants in his garden:
Daphne, stocks, and chrysanthemum.

A poor job was done by the last roofer
And Holy Christ! trouble came in with the rains.
Now it takes a lot of money and pains
To do over what was mucked by that damned loafer.

Chopped great oak and with a big bandsaw
He cut it through a whole June afternoon,
Long as it was from one to seven;
Late dinner and his hands were raw.

It became October: late on an afternoon
He pruned the rose-vine down that bore in bloom
A stock of yellow roses, but the season had turned;
The rose leaves crackled yellow as they burned.

Christmas Day he went to three Masses!
Prayed for the living here and the dead in Ireland,
Gave up thanks for Christ he was glad and the rains at last;
But Christmas like any other day passes.

In May I told him we were having to move;
He said, You've got your own young lives to lead,
That's all right, John. We held four hands together:
We said goodbye then, though we were two months going.

GRADUATE STUDENT

This shield of knowledge
In my one hand,
And in this other
Many a word,
And in between
A welded armor:
Not a chink
Or crack or gap,
All bright plating
Buffed to shining,
Copper bluff
And brazen armor.

Every instant
Sent in action:
Hard rebuttal,
Sharp attack;
Each long hour
One long encounter
Using skills
Of frequent practice:
Killing laughter,
Book and chapter,
Word and stanza.

Into the lists
For name and honors,
High degrees
In the scholars'
Communities,
And a place
Of fame and silver
In another
Warring college.

THIS YEAR LET US REMEMBER WILLIAM BLAKE

(Born 1757: "Now Seven Ages is amounting to Two Hundred Years.")

    The River in its long charge eastward to the sea
    Like an opal vanguard now in its Seventh Age
    From the day of your entry into the vegetating world
    Slides chartered by its stony quays,
    For all your ethos browned with the same filth,
    For all your cries, ribbed by the cruel bridges;
    And Earth has many things to show more fair.

    Where lies the window now through which the cries
    Of your cruel neighbor's boy, shackled in servitude
    To an aching image of your visions of oppression,
    Clapped on your ears like a bugle-call "To the Colors"
    And shot you, bald as Churchill, ruddy as your anger,
    To save that mite of London from his particular blitzing?

    Your houses in Lambeth, Hercules Buildings, or the final
    Fountain Court (great estates, your mental palaces)
    No National Trust Fund saves. They were once weighed
    On the slim side of the silver commercial balance
    And, in their steads, warehouses, shops, and flats
    Occupy the spaces where once walked, sandalled in the gold and
        diamonds of your shining mind
    Your shining and compassionate spirit.

Your Fourfold City is dying, Blake, at the heart of its dying Empire.
It has acknowledged this year your Black Boy grown
Adult in Ghana. India with its tigers teems
Beyond Suez with no heel of a Clive to stamp it down—
There is some progress in two hundred years.
But London, they say, is dying.
And revolt has grown middle-aged in America.
Ah, would you were in your hermitage at Felpham still!

And yet you are. Remembering there, a few breaths from the sea,
I passed your cottage in my mind and saw
John Scholfield clamped in the vises of your fists,
Terror and desperation and compassion
Tight in your squinching eyes, the dust kicked up
All the way from your garden to the Inn,
Recalcitrant as the language or the English nation.
Ah Blake! we can use your hand and your voice still!

Let us forgive him his Loses and Urizens. There is more
Unforgettable in this mighty poet
Than yet we have remembered, the more's our shame.
He was not mad. And less must be forgiven
That shining spirit than often we condone.
This year let us remember William Blake, who was born
Seven Ages ago in Golden Square
And died in seventy years in Fountain Court.

1957

CLASSROOM EXERCISE

Setting out in the lifeboat
captain and 24 men
blue whale sperm or white
here we go after again

Prince Hamlet dodges off
under a billowing pillar
jump him in the surf!
turn the aiming tiller,

pull an oar, Miss Platt!
knuckle down, Nolan,
languid in your seat
you don't pull weight, Miss Dolan.

Deep-hearted seas, brothers,
sisters, oh so deep
under seas smothers
the sweet prince asleep.

"POETRY IN AN AGE OF ANXIETY" *

Beards and long hair recede:
it has been a poet reading,
riding the craft of her words
in a world's hearing.

Now she withdraws her voice
into the small chest
and locket of her breast
and behind her glasses,

and we retreat out doors
that had held the world back,
to stand that suicide attack
(continued light and dark)

which this mad world continues
of homicidal rage,
youthful and barbarous
against our anxious age.

* *A talk by Babette Deutsch at the University of California, Berkeley, October 1958.*

TRIBUTE TO MARK TWAIN

I

Every morning it was clear
young Sam Clemens could see the sun
rise up and shine on a mile of water
stand over the water exactly at noon
move north and south with summer and winter
pass overhead and then slant down
to slam into an unknown ocean.
*But that western ocean became known
and every other under the sun.*

If he looked eastward, where the sun always came from,
surely he saw the long shadows of Longfellow,
Emerson, Holmes, Lowell, the giants of the land
rise up like the loomings of certainty, the tall
and faultless arbiters of Taste,
Destiny, Art, the pilot-marks.

But westward beyond the plains and the mountains
through high hot dusty distances
where water came down from peaks where the driftless ever-
    bodied snow hummed its white dream through an endless
    summer,
their shadows passed underfoot in the dust,
the dust was left behind, and he watched his shadow
under him as he looked down on Tahoe
or riding beside him at his right hand as he came—
nearing fame but not yet having reached it—
riding into San Francisco.

And the river cut them off: they could not walk across water,
Holmes, Emerson, Longfellow, Lowell, Whittier.

II

"Certain southwestern portions" of the human heart
are mapped out here, and claimed,
by Mark Twain, formerly of Hannibal,
formerly known as Sam.

And where the imagination lurks like a catfish
under a shelf of bank, where Sam Clemens
sank, and rose Mark Twain, two fathoms deep
(safe water) and more, the palpitations
of recognizably the central human heart
beat on, beat on. The throbbing paddlewheels
of the sternwheeling heart slap down the river
cruising easy as the dream of youth.

Snags lie ahead, Sam Clemens. *By the mark, twain!*
Before we catch, you lie.

(Great equilibrium
only occasionally secured his mind,
thrown out of kilter, lacking an axle of faith.
Churned by an engine of hope, guided
by a stationary rudder of luck,
the riddled barque *Mark Twain* pulled into port.)

III

And then the sun went down, it was long setting
like the arctic midnight sun, but surely it sank
beneath the sea of doubt. All hope for man
in man's folly went down, titanic.

And in the iceberg: imagine a family
raised on another moral diet—
or, if we lived in another world? But here
we are, in Hannibal again.

And tomorrow is all the same,
a long time coming and a quick time gone,
like when the sun, after a pause at the rim,
rams down in the earth and is gone.

IV

So darkness spread over the face of his mind
and wearing white suits he jested
and summer in linen and winter in serge
white tie and buttons and white-laced shoes
for white is the color of my true love's heart . . .
But under the upshooting ludicrous brows,
a dark look summer and winter in the growing years of his age,
famous and recognized in any quarter of the globe.

On God he never called, but thought
I will go out as I came in
and there, proving him right, was Halley's Comet,
and very soon he set out.

STORM AT EASTER

    Up they come from the South:
        the winds and the mad rain,
from the lands the birds flew to,
        from the lost
    Empires of Spain.

    And the lances of the tall rain
        advance up the plains of the state,
and weapons of the southern wind
        flagellate

each individual man woman and Christ
        of us,
and the breathing bodies and bones
        of all are pierced.

And though this Friday provide
        no proof in hole or blood,
what doubting Thomas could doubt we ride
        the true and original Flood?

THREE SEASONS OF SPRING

This week blossoms appeared on the plum trees
which made in summer a thick wall to our garden
and played all winter in the symphony of twigs
—and the plum trees disappear as if in snow
which seems to have grown whiter every passing
    moment of every day.

But today when I looked at a sprig of the plum tree
I saw that small green leaves are driving
the snowy blossoms away—in a silent,
invisible to the hourly eye, but giant,
mounting, and inexhaustible green blizzard
    slowly covering the boughs.

And underneath the branches these rejected
petals lie, the harvest of early spring,
—small, square, intense, white—
resting on the blades of the long grass
    where the dew sticks them.

Everywhere men are washing their cars.
They think the storms are over
which last week rattled our plum trees
and shook on them a sudden, soft, quick,
evanescent blizzard of blossoms,
    and shook on these the succeeding green.

"BREAK WE OUR WATCH UP"

Look at that linnet, clad in his russet vest:
What's so fresh as he on this spring morning?
He's all chirp; all beginning; all bird.
The world he sees, as he sees, he is creating
Seed after seed, and bug, into song and turd.

What's so fresh as he, at his green post
With sunshine streaming out of his chest?
Only the green morning, his back-drop of fruit-trees
Sidelighted by the nine o'clock sunshine.
And what's spring ever but the year begun?

And what's the year begun, except an image
Of us at our beginnings, as this linnet,
Chirping's the image of spring? And his becoming,
Through a world of flight and air, the image of ours
(Earth-hampered, silent, pedestrian)
Is artifact of nature and history's course.

COLORS OF A CLIMATE

Four colors only are there in Scotland.

First, the grey that is the only constant.
The solid stone burning black as coal into soot,
the solid grey no momentary pall
or smoke from winter-chimneys, or approach
of North Sea mist and fog on an East wind
when the day shuts down.

Second the green that is my Scotland, my Scotland,
spreads into every cranny of land
where the thin rain prances,
springs out of every cleft in cliff or rock,
bears the cities' impatience. Although the Scotsman
thinks his stone and city have crushed it down,
it is not down; but out of any crevice
yearly shoots into life. As each green field
flashes with the riot of blades,
swarms with the points of upward-stinging grass.

Third is the color of flowers. My father plants
who never tilled before, and carefully tends
what grows in the rain, the crystal Standard Rose
that the swinging gale slammed down, the purple
laurel, the various lupins, the royal flag-iris.
And the rhododendrons,
clusters of fire in the countryside,
grow wild in clumps or burnish the local gardens.

And late, late in the sky, at nine o'clock
when my mother goes to bed, before the long
twilight, the red sun
round as a penny falls in the mist,
and there is the fourth color
which I, a stranger in my father's country,
can see in a summer of Scotland, this symphony,
bleeding with stone, savage with fiery plants.

WHOSE PINES ARE THESE?

        Whose pines are these? whose extreme,
        sweet, and pitchy pines? and these
        slender junipers
        and slenderer firs?
        Earth's,
        earth's, are they hers?

BACK FROM UPCOUNTRY
(*Song*)

        I come refreshed.
        Spring in my step.
        It was a cup
        clear in weather
        came to the lip
        of my drinking eye
        and my lungs looked deep.

        I watched the long pines
        pitch the wind.
        Pulled into my head
        odor, and tang
        of sky to my tongue.

        I was drinking long
        and each drop sweet;
        imbibed in the fall
        of autumn weather.

BEAUTY OF A YOUNG MOTHER ON A DAY OF PERFECT CALIFORNIA NOVEMBER

Beauty of her is from her springing free
from the April burden, the baby, in a summer
of wholeness and herself alone again
from sharing that body with her little son.

But she herself is not her only beauty.
It's the child too whose energy is finding
increasing gestures to control
that charms and cheers as he goes on growing.

It will be twenty years before the full harvest.
Meanwhile, as she grows older, is it
memory only I must keep refreshed
of what a beauty there was, in this season

of folded harvests and the spun cocoon?
Or her young beauty, does it not exist
timeless, or younger as the year becomes
older, and as her son assumes his dying?

The small boy bundled is a bound butterfly
who will flap his colors in an April day
equal to this in cool and sun
when California has got over winter again.

EYES OPENED ON AN AFTERNOON

I

Cruelly they have lopped off
The long thin fingers of the elms,
These men with no hearts.
(Though luckily they caught them
In the winter of their feeling.)

II

Rudely awakened from my nap,
I am astonished by mankind.
Can I believe these autos,
These actions, accidents, angers,
These wintered hearts exist?

III

They will sprout again, these fists,
Gestures in a stunted land,
Anger of nature. And I,
Rising at normal morn, will take
Rightly my place on the map of the year awake.

MT. ATLAS CEDARS
(*Cedrus Atlantica*, N. Africa)

>Winter's no wonder for these
>cedars. They wear frost at all times.
>A man could stand under one
>and uphold the world on his shoulders—
>they set the example, standing and
>lifting the sky.

THE WINTER SOLSTICE
(*New Zealand, June*)

I

It is a silent night. In it the moon
Half-full, sliced on the right, slides down the sky,
And the night above me flutters its wings of stars
Like a thrush
           raven-black and flecked with white.
Flat on its plain, the sleeping city admits
The half-moon lurking at the thrush's heart,
And this moon's reflected image appears in streams,
And against the snowed flank of those distant Alps
Where its perpetual night-song echoes.

It is a singing night, in which
The night's thrush-heart peals to the hills
And echoes of daylight gather in every patch
   of pealing water;
Ringing with changes as the winter change
Transforms the plains with frost.
   The wall of peaks opposing
The city which understands no song
Sounds with the din of celestial music,
Attacked by that Joshua of the heavens
Who rings the town with his silver trumpets.

II

There is no native stirring
Whose eyes can comprehend.

Only the alien, tuned
To his strange climate, leaving behind his summer,
Hears it,
       the shining clatter of this moon,

The dulling echo of dim streets and of buildings
Grey and mined of light,
    or the sharp retorts
Puddle and frost and alps return to it.

III

On the mid night of these halcyon days,
The year turns its back and listens ahead
For the coming finches of sunshine;
    turning towards summer;
A deaf ear in the night returned
To the brooding thrush whose egg the moon
Rolls out from her tail
    lopsided down the sky
And will break out of being with daylight,
Shoot from its shell
    the phoenix of morning.
And the ashes of this city pass to ashes,
    And the year moves.

IV

    As I watch,
The speck-breast night broods on the seeded land.
And the frost covers and chills,
    puddle and thatch,
Silvers the ashes of fields and tombstones of roofs.
The mountain echo melts
    and beyond the plain
its trills run down in silence.

The fledgling city sparkles in its nest,
    No tunes in its throat,
    No appetite but hunger.

V

The night grows roaring
    somewhere a radio
a car turns upon shingle
a train is shunted
    a cock crows
    far from morning
a human noise does something
    in the dark
I listen for the moon
    but it is falling.

VI

All continents seem beautiful, but strange.
Yet nowhere the moon echoes wholly in vain
This bright song of the sun.
    Things gain their colors,
To break the day's as the new day breaks the year's
Deep midnight, as the city lightens
Before the dawn returns, before day break;
My silver wonder gilding with delight.

ELEGY

(*for Arthur Jandry*)

In his death, all our deaths are forecast.

And what does the wise man do, to prepare against
Such weather? (Our own bodies cruise
To the same conclusion, like clouds)
To prepare?

Wisely, he took care, and took many cares
Upon him. He lived outside of himself—
He wore his body lightly, as a tree wears leaves,

And bore such an accumulation of tears
That no eye now need weep for such a one,
Who lives most wisely in accumulated honor.

FALLEN HAWK

Crumpled, having come up against too much force,
He who soared and sailed, sovereign of scrub and paddock,
Lies now rolled over, belly and breast up,
The pitch of his present flight directing him
Only darker and firmer downward into the dirt.

An afternoon of warm wind sweeps overhead,
The clouds cry out for companion, the chicks
Mildly await their destroyer. Cars and trucks
Plummet past, a few scarce feet from the claws
That clutched the air and drew the cry of "Hawk!"

Contorted, the wings outspread, but no thin air whines through.
No mourners flock in the trees, it's no cock robin's
Funeral. A massive memorial exists
Only if banked clouds participate,
Piled sky, and burning sun, as monuments.

Small birds and the tiny rabbits rejoice.
It is the dead of winter has seen the death
Of the flier who will not plunder another spring, while,
For the brief degree of their safety, all small things
Do not mourn, crying The hawk is dead!

A RING FROM THE MOUNT OF OLIVES

Returned, a pilgrim, from the Holy Land, you bring
Olive-wood carved by a carpenter
From Christ the Carpenter's olive-green hill.

Is it perfect Jesus you wish me to see in this ring
Of buffed wood, in the pale grain swirled
By the dark brown stain where bore from the bole
A grey branch, like the spume of surf
On a mediterranean world?

Is it your Christ carpenter you wish me to hymn,
Bringing this skillful wooden ring
From the Jews' holy city Jerusalem?
And I join you, join you in Jesus,
If the circling eye of his olive observe
My coming and going, my falling,
Indeed, as closely as the sparrow's?

You have brought me a circle of wood
Turned by a carpenter out of the tree,
While war was tearing the olive boughs
On your holy mount, swiftly as peace.
But I am not saved by his turning
God into man, turned from the living
Olive branch of mercy to a cedar cross
And joined with iron spikes, crowned,
God's ripe berry, with a laurel of thorns.

I play, as I play this ring about my finger,
With the Roman dice as well, I roll them wooden
To knock at the base of this post: to watch
A dog from the multitude come to lift his leg.

YOUNG WIFE AND MOTHER

(for Joy Martyn of Wellington, N.Z.)

>Serenity has composed her. She becomes
>A vessel of warmth in which all else succumbs
>To the impetus of compassion. Now she moves
>Smoothly to the beseech of what she loves
>Across the linoleum of morning, her smile
>Like the shading sun. All the while
>Her mind being full of her duty.
>
>Strange, that devotion genders beauty.

NEW ZEALANDER
(*to Muriel*)

Five Junes ago,
You in your archipelago,
Half the world between
Us, spinning green,
Land and sea reeled through
The slack electric-blue
Air, which, some would claim,
Across us was the same
Sky: which was untrue,
Still, and until the slow
Brain, angling, made it so.

So the fishing winds.
Trading of minds
Across the steam-tracked
Seas joined us, in fact,
Brought you from below
That Equator. So
Well this summer ends,
Making us friends.

1956

TO MURIEL WHEN THE RAINS CAME

The day we were married, it rained.
Ever since has been a flood of blessings,
And today the rain breaks a long spell
Of dry winter, and today the land
Reaches out for its fill.

It's as if we had moved to the tropics!
Here's the monsoon! Here I stand
As if back at the swing-door of my barracks
Looking out through the screen
With a mist of back-spray in my face.
Can it still come faster? How?

Now that you have unlocked the spigot
Of my sex, there is no secret
(It was rust-jamm'd and had been forced,
But to your hand
It turned like a greased shift
Engaged) between us.
And still come down? As if

Winter were a new thing, and Spring
Unheard-of, and Summer to come,
Our drainspout gutters, it does not
Sing, it drums.
And the rain comes.
Somehow we wish to speak our gratitude.
But how?

February 1959

POEM FOR OUR SECOND ANNIVERSARY

My hand before me, my mind hanging back, like our truant
Puppy; and you, rustling and wrapping my present
In the downstairs light for the morning's two
Surprises. And our joy demands I speak:
My mind come forth and rattle my tongue like a clapper,
Toll out a deep telling of our two-year wedding—
And grandly chime to the world the hours of love
That have flocked the wind-lined belfry of our life
Together these hundred and four merry
Blissful Christmas weeks of our gift-given marriage.

Each week ends with a birth. This last of this year's
Climbs to its belltower and leaps, a sheer sound
Into the found, reverberating air
Of our blood in common, issuing a song
Of you, my alive, lover, and forever
Wife of this second, and every year after.

IN RETURN FOR A LOAF

I asked for bread
expecting none—
I had expected
the usual stone;
I had not counted on
this cardboard loaf.

Then there was no fire
crouched on my hearth;
I set out for the store
bought a log in a box
(they said it was oak
—or had been oak—
before it was boxed)
before I was home
it hardened its heart
it ended a brick
of sawdust chip
compressed to rock
(they said it would burn
but it hasn't yet
because in my house
I next found out
the builders left
the hearthstone out
and flames are forbidden
on my hardwood floor).

Wild animals
throng the immense
air overhead
(they say they are birds
but no bird sings)
a world of cats
fights at my door
and giants of dogs

*my daily terror
but it's a long season
since the last hound
or kitten came round
to my garden or rug.*

Now without flames
to turn to toast
a slice or chunk
of cardboard loaf
or dog or kitten
to catch a crumb
what crust do I gnaw
or nourish on?

*I left it three nights
and quick as I thought
that loaf had hardened
to a bleached rock
I thought of wheat
but that's not what
my money bought
it was the wrong crop
I thought about
or flood of falling
and a rare blight
had finished the proper
overnight.*

My wife comes out
with bread in her hands
her hands have made
her hips are loaves
newly browned
crusts crunch
wherever she steps
and little dogs follow
to swallow them up.

*This is my body,
her lips said,
broken for you,
where animals feed,
this is my body
and this is my blood
is what I remember.
This is my love.*

SUITS FOR THE DEAD: POEMS

By DAVID R. SLAVITT

Copyright © 1961 David R. Slavitt

For Lynn

I

SESTINA FOR TEA TIME

More than the words of a conversation, the taste
sticks to the tongue, like frozen metal. The tea
we drink from these pottery cups turns the room
into some precious Swinburnean relic, the mind
adding its own flavor. Just the idea
of tea is a leaf you cannot filter out.

I think of Turgenev, his elaborate tea set out,
the sugar held in the teeth as an idea
is held in the mind (and the idea takes on the taste
of the sugar). Or I think of a blue and gold room
and Madame de Staël, sipping the mind
of some great gentleman, as we sip tea.

And I think of the Brontës, somehow, as always at tea.
Lapsang-souchong, or jasmine each has its taste,
so is there a flavor to each idea
which is blended into the cup or is strained out.
This afternoon, this tea, us, this room
could become, in time, a part of the taste of the mind.

That the words will be gone is nothing, for somehow the mind
retains the faces, furniture, as just a taste.
Good talk goes with tea, and years later the tea
still tastes of that talk. It is not unlike the idea
of conversation with the words left out—
as of lovers, say, at last alone in a room.

A glass of beer at night, thus, may turn a room
into some fictive Heidelberg, where the mind
gets drunk, and the body stays sober. The taste
of Hegel, for instance, has nothing to do with tea
unless you studied him in England—out
of such irrelevant circumstances an idea

acquires physique, becomes sensible; and an idea
needs this to survive. It may live in tea
longer than in books, and come to mind
one afternoon, suddenly filling the room
when you were sure that intellect had stepped out
and you were left alone with feeling and taste.

An old friend, an idea, should have a room
where it can visit, somewhere out of the mind,
in the house of taste, perhaps, with a cup of tea.

AS TRUE AS I STOOD

As true as I stood
in midwinter air, hearing the bells chime
so clear that they clappered into my chill blood
tart and sublime,

I have wished sincerely
to send on that numbing air a like rime
even if it, too, were to sound less and less clearly
with distance and time.

If delight the bells give,
always becoming, is always disappearing,
and sound leaks through mind like rain through a great sieve
and is soon out of hearing,

a man—or some boy—
then yanking the rope out of duty and all his breath
had no time for time, ringing the bell in his joy,
nor was bothered by death.

AT ST. TROPEZ

Naked on the Tahiti Plage
beyond the last umbrella cluster, the last
white pedallo, they lie at the end of the beach
or swim in the blue water, continuous gold,

while planes chartered from Ste. Maximime
at a hundred and fifty feet buzz breasts, behinds,
return and are gone, having brought and taken
the high aesthetic purity of voyeurs

undisturbed by the long glare
that blurs the honest lechery of yachtsmen
anchored opposite, their glasses sweeping the field,
to the abstract love of an ornithologist.

And a man sits with a yellowy Pernod
and stares out at the port at the end of the day,
having seen them lie in the sun on the belly of Europe
all afternoon, the last people on earth.

KNICK KNACK

Ceramic head high, held as to sniff the air
when some brush crack and sudden hush in the trees
has chilled the soft pine woods to nerves and sunlight,
the knick-knack horse, survivor of a pair,
stands among cup-and-saucer equerries
as tame as toast, ingratiating, slight.

It was in fire that such white was bred,
a ghast-white glaze; and fire in his nature.
He traffics on the wild plains of the head.
O there is grace in him in limb and stature
for which some town might well tear down its wall.
Laocoön proclaimed his worth: enjoy
the horse, so sinister—though very small—
pawing the earth before a teacup Troy.

MUSICIAN AT COURT

The infanta's dreams reigned, in some other kingdom,
while he played sonatas upon a gilt harpsichord,
not paying attention, like her, in a private thralldom.
The courtiers were even perceptibly bored.
The infanta, at moments, would listen to what she heard,
raising an eye or a fingertip, and he
would repeat the passage without saying a word,
nod—not to her, but to rhythm—and would reflect
on matters of counterpoint and polyphony,
and how disparate themes will sometimes intersect.

A PERSON FROM PORLOCK

    We patronize this man, famous, nameless
    (assuming it was a man), or we become
    righteous and full of academic rage
    which is too easy,
    pretending to thirst for that last third of a page
    that Coleridge might have written, if that dumb,
    that absolutely oafish, and yet quite blameless
    (I think of him as breezy.)

    person from Porlock whose business ought to have waited
    hadn't knocked, had known that the rather quizzical
    old poet was off on one of those binges.
    Still, let us delight
    that the world of Porlock—or Jackson Heights—impinges
    a little on Khan, on Coleridge. The metaphysical
    Fullerbrush man's knock, though sometimes hated,
    is somehow right.

I HAVE NO PRAISES

I have no praises for these prospective crones
Although the interest has not centered yet
To a cameo on onyx, or a clip, or a jeweled lorgnette,
Their maiden forms still pendant from straight bones.

My scorn for these girls, yearning with every kiss
To catch themselves a man, with a tidy figure,
But O the songs I'd sing, bright Artemis,
If you were palpable as they, and half as eager.

COMES TO THE HOLLOW

        Comes to the hollow of a girlish heart,
        soft and strong as a new grown boy,
        a quiet instant, salt with grief,
        and her eyes close, and her lips come apart.

        And hours later, one will say,
        "Life is bitter," or "Life is sweet,"
        or perhaps beg pardon for drifting off,
        remembering her that way.

PARTITI DA COTESTI CHE SON MORTI

Unrehearsed, for the love of laughing, her laughter gushed;
the wind pressed her skirt to her thighs for the love of spring;
and there I was, with her, in a laughing springtime,
when the year's first life of blood and kisses rushed.

Full of the devil and heavenly hopeful, I came
with prayers and oaths and offerings—devoted novitiate.
But I learned my love, and she was a hard mistress.
O, a school girl can be such a wise old dame.

She returned my smiles. I put my books away,
and loved till my lips were chapped. Then was the time
for notes and whispers. To hell with the old professor!
"Never forget the footnotes," he used to say.

This I remember: she was false as the lunatic sea.
The tide went out and billowed away to God
knows where, with a furious salty good bye.
On the beach I still find bits of the old debris.

That clip at her throat, gleaming in half light,
hair with lavender scent, a black scarf—
out of my mind! I want no relics. Go
after her. Go, wish her a good night.

WARNING

First, beyond all
song, or any note,
was that terrible small
silence in her lovely throat—
and all along,
the quiet potency for
most fantastic song.

Still, there lingers
in Philomela's cries
the echo of her deft fingers
when her music flies.
She could not sing
except for outraged muteness,
Procne, and the king

who had his wild will.
You, who would make bold,
beware when they keep still.
The tale is old:
quiet as snow,
a heart will burst—then warble
when the mind lets go.

IN THE SERAGLIO

The maharani of midnight tresses,
jaded, silvered, and rustling silk,
smiles at her eunuchs and undresses,
bathes, and her black hair floats in milk,

bathes and listens (a woman sings;
others play musical instruments),
emerges, and a servant brings
dusting powders and frankincense.

A dozen virgins, brought to serve
the maharani in her mood,
dry her with kisses; their smooth lips curve
with a sweet and tingling lassitude.

The maharani's half closed eyes
swim in their tawny bodies' grace.
She touches one of the delicate thighs
to delight in the blush on another's face.

(Thus had the maharani blushed
as the maharajah's fingers swept
over her body once and brushed
away the tears that she had wept.)

She kisses the naked, blushing girl
whose breasts are sharp and whose mouth is tart,
honey and jet and mother-of-pearl.
She holds the girl tight to her heart,

then sends her to the great lord's bed,
and pulls the girl with the delicate thighs
down on the cushions, a-tremble with dread
while the others hide their eyes.

AFTER THE JAPANESE

    It has been six days
    and still she cannot touch
    four small flowers
    wilted in a glazed white jug.

TO AN ESCORT OF AN HONEST LADY

Walking in leafkicking time over the tweed hill,
handswinging sunward for the late day's cool,
and feeling the underfoot earth tighten and chill,
she may neglect her etiquette and the rule
and will not say she loves you more than another,
yet do not praise or pity or take her to task
when you see her turn to you, as she must, and ask
you, "Please, please, keep me from the February weather."

SMALL BIRDS

Small birds, calling out of their hungered fright
perched on the swaying of a moonlit brambled space
over the scurry and scamper of tiny sight
themselves under great soaring of lethal grace,
silver the air with a particular chill and sheen.

I know those birds that whimper when shadows start,
the glazed eyes, peering. I have seen
that fluttering dread in my love with her small bird's heart.

LEPIDOPTERAN

All little legged bugs that buzz, that fly,
or silent, sweep by her hair or beat on the screen,
beetle slick, hairy, or furry, terrify

her: but moths most, with wings in a blurred sheen
and butterflies that send her arm-waving and crying.
Of course, it's psychological (Psyche seen
as butterfly, her luminescence flying
out of the heads of the dead. *Athanaté
hai psyché*—but the legend seems to be dying).

And for her fears, there is little that one can say
who cannot see those bright souls in the air
wing'd from the blessed isles, or the moths, grey

Stygian shades, longing for lights. They bear
all tombstones with them on their pallid wings.
She cries aloud. Her hands cover her hair.

Her butterflies and moths are furious things.

ON A PLOT, 50 x 100

Snow on the backs of pink lawn flamingos
betrays them painted metal, and gives the lie
to summer's housewife by whose ordering eye,
that law unto the lawn until it froze,
those birds were posed, patrollers of her grass.

Yet she will sweep her fiction in the snow,
as good as new, and as the winters pass,
lean on her broom, and dare those birds to go.

*

      star
      fish on the floor
      of oceans are
      lovely, lovely more
      than sapphire or pearl,
      or cast
      on silent beaches
      asterisks to a past
      that each point reaches:
      forgotten animated swirl.

      known
      by children on sand
      who prod in wonder
      ponder by hand
      is the intricacy under
      the brown
      echinoderm:
      impulse and motion
      lately held firm
      in folds of ocean.

BLOCKS

At random playing and by accident,
having set two blocks, the small hands take a third,
place it across—and those two have become
posts and this third suddenly a lintel.
A gate! an arch! a door! An elemental
awe: here, without any bugle or drum,
free of distraction from any chiseled word
he looks upon the towering monument

to the simple setting of thing on thing: abstract
but undeniable structure. The enclosed space
is charmed, is holy. The hand is held in wonder
and fear of touching that third inviolate
block crowning the simple new-made gate.
The world is divided into an over and under,
and all is in or out. And at this place
all quadrants and divisions meet, exact,

where the marker marks itself, where on the floor
the child prone, peers through the opening
fixed on nothing, the nothing at all at the center,
space beneath the one block and between two
(a miracle, which he is learning is his due,
like the first summer after the first winter),
No mere and general marvelings at the thing—
but a corkscrew staring into the empty core.

BALLOON

Even two years is plenty of downwardness,
the tiresomeness of it, the boring sameness of weight.
That the block with the zebra on it, splendidly flipped
with a speculative off-hand side-arm more or less
toss should not, even briefly, hesitate
but fall like a sedulous clerk, obedient, whipped

is an outrageous waste of perfectly good possibility.
Imagine, then, this too-blue picture postcard
day, with the animals loping or sleeping in sun
and the air not cold but crisp with the civility
of good servants, walking from lions toward
okapis, gnus, giraffes, and coming upon

this not-quite-picturesque-enough person with his
overpriced ice-cream, his crackerjax, and for the first
time in your entire life, balloons which stand
up. Up! A haircut at Best's is
all one could want, but the balloons they hand out are the worst
droopers and fallers and danglers from your hand—

But these, most marvelously balanced on their strings,
these beautiful blue zoo hallucinations
of the crew-cut and alas, un-Italianate vendor
sway with the wind: not mere imaginings
but real things of the real world on vacations
from its gross, grey gravity, or on a bender

with only a single strand left of sobriety
as though they were rid of their shoes, but encumbered by
the still recalcitrant laces. Familiar with jumping
on the big double bed, for example, and filled to satiety
with the creak of springs, the pillows' obesity,
the flatness of mattresses, bathos, the bore of clumping

back down, I bought one of the balloons
green and giddy with gas, and brought it home
to watch it nose the ceiling like a goldfish,
only to see it lose that afternoon's
buoyancy, decline and fall, like Rome,
with that tired grace that is the final wish

of all extravagant high living. Back at the zoo
having felt that sweet tug at my finger,
I should have let it go and lived its flying.
It would have been the humane thing to do.
But you ignore the elephants, don't you, and linger
 to share the captive platypus's dying.

GREAT GRANDFATHER

"Non sai tu che tu se' in cielo?"

The world is a blur in his cataracted eyes,
as he rocks in nostalgic obscenity.
Too warm for worms, too cold for the flies,
he reels off the names of his progeny.

He has fathered sons who have fathered sons,
and has long been done with fathering,
though the girls still quake where his young blood runs,
and his is all but the bothering.

Milk from the udders of unknown cows
goes pouring down his gullet,
and he sits, and his billowing memory blows
over spawning schools of mullet.

No one knows what he's thinking of.
Nobody knows if he's thinking.
Reciting the names that have come of his love,
he sits in the sunshine, blinking.

IRT

He was a big man
came into the subway car
and tall

very tall
so that the woman standing beside him
looked up to the knot of his tie
and broad

broad as a bull in a blue silk suit
and everyone there who sat in the crowd or stood
thought What a big man

God what a
big man.

PRESTO

>Quick, as the crow
>flies black over snow
>and is gone
>silent and clean,
>black over the white
>is black over the green
>in the night
>that the crow flies on.

CHANTEY

The sailors sing a lovely song
to celebrate the gulls
that eat the fish then swim along
drowned sailors' smiling skulls.

Delight in the fitting of tune and word,
delight that thought can stray
to the abstract grace of flying birds
over so many fathoms of bay.

EARTH HATES AN EMPTINESS

Earth hates an emptiness as a woman hates
a wasted seed, though the weight of a household
is more to bear than the barren frame, or the old
cellar hold where dirt accumulates.
More than the imminent end or the actual fall,
more than the funerary chimney stones, the mess
of the last crumblings, earth hates an emptiness,
for, though afterwards, there is nothing left at all,
this deepest offense is greatest—unnatural signs
of pure *posse,* music merely on the page,
a house come to the ghostliness of its age
in a wilderness of celibate pumpkin vines.

NO SARABAND

No saraband without its capriol;
never pavan
sans galliard. Thus the dance
figures Hamlet's hyperion
antiphon
to satyr inheritance

All things in time: low bow of Caliban
must soon adjourn
to the lavolta air of Ariel.
Prospero's proper concern
is the turn
from wine goblet to bell.

The players, dancers, change with the changing measure
musicians play,
verging on mummers' magic:
Hamlet's dumb show is gay
in the way
Prospero looks to the tragic.

The play, as the play-within-the-play, is done;
the curtains kill,
quicken corpses, seal the show,
drawing the Hamlet and the Prospero
together and still
in what they both know.

IN HIS OWN COUNTRY

You, Mendel Beilis, Jew to us,
as if, say, old Samson had come to sit
in a Bronx delicatessen, eating salami,
reminiscing of how it was in Gaza;
absurdly biblical, you, martyr of the Concourse,
no distant Shadrack, but (marvelous!) mere Mendel,
come, at the last, to a corner where mothers sit
telling their children of you ("See *mein kind,*
the man of God who walks with a folded Forvitz
across the street."),
                you, Beilis (Job
does not nibble chocolate halvah in the park!),
who wallow in the world, profounder than Plato
and subtler than Jesus, you, genial old man,
you ask too much.
                Your awing us at all
must awe us most: we weep to see you doze
or feed the pigeons in our afternoons.

DE BELLO

    Little of late will focus:

    these thinkers, while the dailies moan, proceed
    apologizing for the civil war
    past all remembrance, and Sarajevo
    unexplained, and the Danzig question—
    Too much, already, and the threat of more
    makes study urgent, which is unbecoming,
    and beggars all accounts of Malvern Hill.

    Let us consider Caesar (lucid Latin),
    construe the Gauls, and reason the campaigns.
    For tribute. F.O.B. SPQR
    Which gives it a reason, tit for tat, bug in a rug,
    yet reason—within reason. Something of choler,
    something of melancholy, yet clearly sane.

    But Tamburlaine. And Khan. And the Corsican
    still sets those scholars working, who would find
    cause and effect within the saber's compass,
    Pin Gettysburg upon a hanging map . . .

    O think of Pickett! Life is streaming out.
    Life *is* the streaming, red on the grey, the green.
    That little war, or others; and all others.

    The reading is no better for the light
    of high Troy burning.

CERBERUS

The thunderhead of the dogday's night
fringed with ermine, mooncrossing slowly,
bearing its ancient, rere regardant,
breaks the formation, hovering lovely
with a havoc cry and a shower of might,

falls on the country, whelms the village.
Townsmen take cover, leaving only
the yellow dog, the yellow dog
drenched in the street, mad and lonely,
chasing his tail through all of the pillage.

Frantic, chaotic, his holy brain
full of the road dust, lightning, water,
the mongrel dog on a mongrel night
blind and brighteyed, running harder,
spewing saliva into the rain . . .

and then a retreat of the thunderhead.
The townsmen resume their careful careers,
remark that the storm has finally gone,
but even though no trace appears
of the yellow dog, he is not dead.

In a cave hidden in a secret glen,
the oldest boulders hide him away,
asleep, while his quivering jaws are keeping
all their fury for a dreadful day
when the ancient dog will storm again.

TAUB

He uses a good worsted, Taub does,
nothing fancy, but good honest fabric,
and makes real button holes. His suits for the dead
are good looking, good suits. He made a joke
(there isn't any back to a dead man's jacket),
saying once, "I stand behind my suits."

He listens to music, loves his wife and children,
and lately has begun to do pastels:
flowers arranged in a wide blue bowl, or fruit
with a richness of reds in with the yellows and greens.
But he takes his pride in his business, and his art
is button holes—the real button holes.
"Out of respect. A man deserves that much."

MEDITATION

"We are," he said, "more saintly than Francis, for we
lecture to stones," and we laughed, and I thought of the stones
and rocks he had meant, of Shakespeare, and I thought
of those others *Bleste be ye man yt spares thes stones*
and wondered what's in a stone.
                          We long for them
for they are long in time and longer than wonder
that the child feels finding one sudden morning
when he has learned to reckon that this clock
and that chair, say, and all those spoons
are older than he and know the prior world
where he was not.
               Amazing as the rattle
of his growing, sucked and stared at, held or flung,
is this his ageing to knowledge of age. And stones
are old, standing in graveyards, greyer than brains,
and we are as silent with them as he with pebbles
held in a pink hand feeling them hard.
He clicks them together, throws them far, far, far . . .
who will think, awake, in a sweet good-nighted room
of the safe, dumb stone, under a bush
and be sad.
        He:I.
              And envious
because it is smooth or round or rough or shaped,
but hard, harder than any head that knows it.
I have heard tell of the painter's fear of canvas,
bare and stupid; even more the sculptor,
before that hulking silence, dreads the stone.

APOLOGY

When the mind soars cadenzas into an airless aerie
fomenting visions shaped to a cancrizans
chameleon colored, the color of fair waters
fountaining in the arcade under lights, then
stop: the creation is a chaos of disgrace
that I am reduced to such and such paltriness
who have once mischiefed grandly, nor can forget
a poem is, after all, only a poem,

and hands have held better than pencils, and lips more than words,
and mind has done more than this chewing upon itself
nor would so now, but the Ravager's "got culture"
and keeps to "less neiges d'antan" in a cozy library—
while the real snow and the chill of its old day
are all gone—sparing what can be well spared . . .
not that I dislike literature, but then,
a poem is, after all, only a poem,

and yet beautiful because extravagant, (denying
the author's nose-itch, a reader's ulcer
and the printer's club-foot) hanging like geometry
on an insubstantial point—no thing. The shame
is upon me, that a full-muscled man should be playing thus
at ratiocination causeless, ineffectual, that mind
is its own recluse with none but the feeble, final
excuse: in your hand, on this page, here, now.

SONNET: WITH INTERLUDE

Stammer of pen came first, or all at once
they came, with that first evident (no clinician,
white-coated, gauged, with mirror to the mouth,
but knows to look beyond the lip that trembles
and drools with trying). My brain stammers, and soul
and I am a crow, slit-tongued, and rasp with effort.

    Humility: my master taught it me;
    Old Fitts gave up the genie (and the bottle)
    out of a kind of meekness. Carmelites
    must bless that ear as fine as any living,
    his wildness, his control, his precious wits
    that still play on the Greek I never learned.
    Great men have written; Dudley will be dumb
    and honor them (. . . and seyde O deere childe
    I halse thee . . .)

    Dignity: I learned this by myself;
    my age, degrees, career, and fatherhood
    all bid me comb my hair of poetry
    and, silent, watch my son who crows for joy
    of noise, and smile a condescending smile,
    the same for Yeats' monkey glands, the possum's
    quail, Pound sprung at the hatch, the scandalous
    heart, Crane, and darlin' Thomas (even
    the Miller's tail). Disgraceful!
                        O but splendid!

Paul Weiss this year has set himself aesthetics,
begun to paint, to write, sculpt, dance, and sing—
my friend, professor, and philosopher,
full fifty, father, widower, and wise!

And I must stop to listen, laugh, and marvel
at this chirping owl, announcing perpetual dawns
till I forget myself in my stammering age,
and ageless, prideless, proud, find in him voice.

CLASS POEM
(Delivered at Yale University, June 10, 1956.)

Here, in this pleasant space, this easy time,
into the pride and pathos of this day,
I come before you, with my sober rime,
knowing you may not like what I must say;
I have no wish to anger or repel,
yet you may take ill how I wish you well.

I cannot pray for general success:
prayers have their own, particular direction.
All I can give in such a public address
is all I have—a mere and private affection.
Who wishes more may have all he can earn—
the poem's mine; the matter's your concern.

If you are learned, then you must be wise,
sparing of speech, easy and discreet;
a pompous learning is the worst fool's guise—
the braying serves to make the ass complete.
I would remind those of the scholarly clan
that learning is but the footnote to the man.

You who would try the alchemy of art
must be most wary of this: should you succeed,
then of alchemic guilt within the heart,
or, should you fail, then of the gold you'll need.
But regardless of how well you invoke the muse,
good art cannot a wretched life excuse.

A camel may get through a needle's eye
when they build bigger needles. Until then,
those who'd amass great fortunes before they die
must remember the words about heaven and wealthy men.
It is often forgotten by Madison Avenue grads
that Life is not a collection of New Yorker ads.

Know learning, art, and wealth are accidents,
things men of substance neither crave nor spurn,
peripheral to that central excellence,
which if you do not know, you cannot learn.
So drink this down with your fine Mory's ale:
you are not saved for having gone to Yale.

All I have said, you all have heard before.
I warn you now, do not forget it later,
lest Yale, which is—and can be—something more,
fade to "Old Blue," "Bulldog," and "Alma Mater."
My valediction then: 'It's understood
Yale men do well; may some of you do good.'

II

II

JERICHO

"You could see the river from camp; you could climb a tree
or stand on a high rock and stare at it
and beyond to the valley and hills that stretched west
until your eyes swam—not from emotion
but with an unblinking dumbness, for this was the end
of all the pitching and breaking of camp, of marching,
of praying, of making up songs. You do not believe
in the column of fire, of course, and the column of cloud,
but these are ways of describing the kind of faith
we all had, and you who were not there
must imagine in these unlikely ways the feeling
of high purpose, the sense of history, the pride
that the old man could breathe into us again
and again even for forty years.
                                              At the end,
in sight of the river, everything fell apart,
and all of us felt old and acted young,
and the camp was a mess, and there were fights and more fights
and one man got his eye put out, and another
got his foot chopped off with a cleaver and bled to death.
The generals issued orders, of course, and priests
summoned us for sermons and for prayers,
but there was an epidemic of dysentery
and there was all the talk that the old man
was going to die, that he had said himself
that he never expected to make it across the river,
which, as I said, you could see from where we were.
So the orders and the sermons all went for nothing,
and at night the men would go off to Shittim and the whores.
We waited there in the spring rains and the mud
that showed our footprints, aimless as kept cattle,
until the news came back from the mountain to camp
that Moses was dead, and the soldiers wept and the women
were quiet; I remember the trite sound
of the shouting of children playing at some game
in the thin sunshine.

                    I thought, 'This is the end,'
and even felt relief, as at a play
whose ending I could see and appreciate,
applauding the splendid spirit of the venture,
savoring ironies in its near-success.
There was a rightness to it which I sucked at
as at the sweetness of a decaying tooth,
all through the prayers and eulogies for Moses,
and through the following morning when I was called
to report for orders. They sent us across the river,
two of us—me and Isaacson—as spies.

                            * * *

There was a time I wept for Jericho,
the odd streets, loud with the cries of hawkers,
the smells of cooking, even those famous walls
which were touched with pink at sunset and then turned grey
with shadows from the turrets black as velvet.
Later, after moonrise, silvered shapes,
huger than clouds, they rode the plain.
                                        I wept
for those walls once, and for the people in them
dead because it was somehow inconvenient
that the city was where it was, and that our plans
made no allowance for the fact of their existence.
But I have outgrown that old rage. Killing
is easy, is nothing. How simple it would be
to kill a man—for profit, say—and be done with it,
run your sword through his belly: you could repent
and lead an exemplary life, and be saved or damned.
But we were the chosen people, and God's will
was the dirty business we acted out
and feeling free all the time—as free as the birds
that fly, chirping and singing, north and south
spring and fall, stupid and automatic.
We entered the city at night, dressed as shepherds.
The streets smelled of manure, shops were still open
and I remember a bracelet set with garnets

that I admired. And in the taverns laughter,
talk of the day's prices, stories, complaints.
We walked the streets, cautious at first, then glad
just to be in a city.

* * *

                        At the change of the watch
we went to a whore-house, sat with the clerks, the soldiers
a couple of old merchants, a few farmers,
and heard the talk, which was of Israel,
the kingdoms we had conquered, and the sea
that opened for us, and then, closed, drowning them.
Even the girls were afraid, standing together
at one end of the room, talking of the rapes
they thought we had committed. Now and then,
one would pass among us, stroking hair,
sitting on a lap or smiling, trying
to drum up business while there was time, hoping
the talk of disaster might loosen purses, wanting
to die, if she had to die, at least with some money.
To celebrate these signs of our power, proud,
we obliged, and went up with Rachab, to her room.
Naked, she looked at us naked, and melted with terror
to see that we were circumcised, were Jews,
were part of the army of Israelites. She became
suddenly a different kind of woman,
who would not take our money, who made love
helplessly, who trembled throughout, afraid
not of what we might do but of who we were,
and later, begged for her life.
                        One of the maids
had also seen us, had found us out, had reported
to one of her soldier friends who came with guards,
but Rachab hid us up on the roof, and lied
boldly to the soldiers, asking only
that we spare her life, when we came to take the city.
Remember, we two were the first of all Israel
to stand in the promised land. And Rachab's awe

I felt, myself, but later. And her fear.
Then I despised her as simply a traitorous whore,
which, I suppose she was, but that whore's couch
was as good an altar as any I have seen
to the power of God. Never mind blessing Him,
keeping His laws, praying, but understand
that He gave us a country, and that He took it away
from the people who lived there, as a capricious cat
might keep its tit from a kitten and let it starve.
Believe in the world only, and in fortune,
and follow good luck, and pay respect to money
and this is recognition of the Lord
and reverence for His works. And of course, whoring.
We exchanged protection, and she helped us escape
and we fled to the hills northward, where we hid
while she, I suppose, went about her business
taking on clerks and soldiers and fat merchants
and waiting for our return, and her city's fall.
After three days, we made it back to camp,
gave our report, and were commended for it,
and the rest you know—how we attacked the city
and blew our horns, and saw the walls fall down.
The whole absurd story . . .
                    Gambling men
in a like fashion throw their chip on the cloth
and win with their eyes closed to show the world
that their luck is running, and the croupier
pays just the same, and the sensible men at the table
shrug their shoulders and place their bets with the winner,
riding his luck. So Rachab was saved,
was accepted into our tribe, and we went on
to conquer the people of 'Ai, and all the land
that God promised us.
              At Jericho
we stood before the walls with those silly trumpets
and that same year, far to the northwest,
barbarians stood before Troy, (I hear with a horse)
and they too won a victory, and made up
their own absurd story—which is right,
and the only way to explain an absurd thing.

* * *

The land is ours now, and I plow my field,
but the terror I saw in the eyes of that girl is mine,
for the way we won was not any human way,
and I do not pee in running streams, I avoid
hunchbacks, I put on my left shoe first.
We stand here on our little eminence
and study to construe God's subtle laws,
but the column of cloud was thunder visible,
and the column of fire was obvious enough.
A row of sunflowers stands on the edge of my field,
and I watch them watch the sun, turning to westward
as the sun turns, and I have often wondered
whether the flower hates the thing it thrives on,
indifferently burning down life and decay.
Still, we could not have ignored those holy tokens
back in the desert, or found our way by ourselves."

ACTAEON

I

No nasty Tom, but with loud horns and yelping
in honest hunt, Actaeon in that wood,
come to a clearing, saw the goddess naked,
she and her maidens, laving in a pool—

and still, no light, no multifoleate rose,
nothing of supernature
                        but washing women.
"Cognosce dominas tuas!"?
                    "Cave canes!"?
                                Posted?
nothing,
        but rustle of green leaves over them,
and rush of water blue in afternoon
and wet limbs gleaming in the sprinkled sunlight.
So hid he then, the hero in that wood
within a thicket, innocent as they
and gay for the adventure
                            (as Anchises
was with Aphrodite who asked only,
"Do not go bragging at your feasting tables
nor whisper privily in the small hours,
nor tell to any man that, 'Aphrodite
was my Aeneas' dam. I tupped a goddess . . .' "
This he denied and was struck down most sorely.)

and still by Gargaphie's pool was no betrayal,
but only beauty swimming in his eyes.

II

Granting injustice, we must grant also
the teeth tearing the flesh, the cries of comrades,
where is Actaeon? words (his friends' teeth) snapped

as all rushed to the kill, and grant his death
—more lively than a picture gallery,
for here was no carved marble—a rare find,
who have no beauty for ourselves to die in,
no birdsong loud enough to break the drum.

Hiding in the bush it was mere vision,
until the watersplash, when all her beauty
tickled down his neck. Front to front,
mortal and goddess, bank and pool, wet,
both:
   me miserum dicturus erat.
And we must grant it all, then, knowing nothing,
who sleep through dawns, and who forget death
lurking in sunsets that must be **followed** boldly.

Allow then passion in the sprouting antlers
where verba animo desunt; fear the dogs
running the rough stigmata in their jaws.

III

(Two Interruptions)

Loeb Librarian:

"Now, go and tell," or words to that effect
(it is important that we take the event in context)
thus was he baptized, thus the horns
budded above the ears, verba desunt
sic—according to most reliable accounts
with which any interpretation must come to terms.
Truth is a tricky business. Ask Aquinas.

Sincerely, Thomas:

Having been perceived by mortal eye,
her Truth-in-the-understanding suffered change,
for she, Diana Trivia, was seen
who, before, had not been seen, had been unseen.
Hers was a metamorphosis of a kind,

devolving from Actaeon, whose quick change
was only fair then. Thus a kind of union:
he and Diana, virgo. Poet, take notice.

IV

He and Diana: considering them, we
must follow with the huntsmen in the chase,
must stand with the attendants in the pool,
witnessing leaves in the wind, the clouds, riding
random in the usual sky, the visible
hills far off, the earth under our feet:
background, understanding background only.

We cannot even say with a certainty,
"There was something . . . I remember something
in the quiet afternoon . . ."
                                and yet, we saw,
not knowing enough of love to call these "lovers,"
(the burden of miracles is for the observers)
the sudden change: man into mute stag.
Wholely transparent, purer than crystal, invisible,
nothing betrayed them to us. A stately change:
as, by a thought, a bowl on a potter's wheel
becomes a vase—sudden and yet with grace:
as Zeus was a swan, a bull, a golden shower,
Actaeon
        was a stag.

ORPHEUS

Floating his lifeless head, the river ran
that once had shimmered still to his living song,
bobbed it in current, rolled it in running water,
and the head of the charmer, singer, Orpheus, silent
as the death that washed it, suddenly, lively sang.
Then, as a stream of water, a stream of music
coursed through his brains, as blood flowing like crystal.
    I have lived there; have made in my own ghostliness
    Hades, Persephone, 'live in my lyre's moment,
    quicken to melody—performed all this easily
    as I have turned stags into the shades of my music.
The river sang all along out of mouth and source
from the speck in the water to river bank and wood
and mountains away, in ranges of audience,
heard the heart in the head, beating its notes out of silence.
The joy of singing sang to the theory of song:
no one to no one, of mathematics and air.
The floating wonder spun along the water
while the trees held still to listen that they could dance.
    My song outlives me, having charmed the furies.
    There is no death, and they will sing it always
    having heard it once. I, I am the singer,
    maker, master. Deathless, I am the song.
His head floated down the river and into the sea
where the currents caught it and carried it to Lesbos
and the waves washed it up on a sandy beach.
And there, covered with brine and caked with sand,
the head of Orpheus, spectacle for sea birds,
lying on its side, bodied by driftwood—
there, still, the head in its spirit sang
prophesies, oracles, far and wild on the winds.
    Real as my music, alive as all that hear me,
    I sing my testament in simple phrases:
    Godless, whatever I choose, I can make immortal,
    unnatural and worldly by my lyre.

There was no body now for head to turn on,
and all the landscape, forward, in it, singing
out of his mouth, flooding his ears and eyes,
bloomed in his voice. Eurydice had blossomed
into that landscape, out of the shadows by music:
her cheek had reddened, eye had glistened again,
brighter at every note. Her flowing shroud
unravelled as her blood ran to his song.
    Singing Eurydice, Eurydice,
      I brought her all that way to breath itself,
      beyond that kingdom—even beyond my song,
      where, for a moment, again, the sun could glimpse her.
But Orpheus—turning around, away from his strains,
for only a moment—seeing the sun again,
the miracle possible and amazing, turned
back to look as if his eyes were needed;
when all the world was watching, fixed in wonder,
wondered, himself, and turned out of his singing,
and time rumbled and turned again on its axis
to spin Eurydice out into silence and haze.
    "Farewell," she called, vanishing to air,
    and I called into empty air, "Farewell."
    And now, full of grief, I sing how it wás póssible
    and rooted trees have been moved to hear my lament.
Angered Apollo repaired and silenced the corpse
whose head stayed tides at the flood in boundless singing,
but afterwards he wept for his dissonant son,
bereft of the world, and out of all its order,
the shining Orpheus, returned to the grey land
where music is enough. He drank of Lethe
who once had sung, in a river that could not hold him,
and loud into the ears of the sleepy world.

HOMAGE TO LUIGI BOCCHERINI

I

Landon to Haydn's Roosevelt, Luigi
Boccherini also ran
                    bows over strings
made minor music poor (I mean unmoneyed)
and died poor.

Melody, child of a pennywhistle mind,
brings out the warbler in us, chirruping seagull,
the color of jays, gay and gliding:
all laud and honor then from the dancing dons
that whistle across the court, and pay ye all homage
to Boccherini and his singing like.

Not the common man; not great, nor near great,
nor "for trying" but ipse, good as he was,
musician, music (i.e. of the muse),
and in that thrall—like to a priesthood,
                            like to a disease . . .
That mind could pulse the heartbeat, fleshed and ringing,
praise Boccherini, awful and abstract.

II

I have heard that agile playing
in drowsy claret afternoons,
poised upon some fragile word
of mine, or drifting on his tunes,
and loved as he was close to me
and trembled at his violin.
Boccherini, peerless, plays
the dancing shadows' coming in.

III

"Poet, make up your miracles, work your wonders:
that epic sop: tell him your blood is his:
journey: blind, crazy, club-foot, or drunk:
harrow again, or climb the mountain and ask

What world is this of yours? what thing this music?

and make him speak as you have found him out."

But intervals of voices in the hearing,
in the world's hearing, faint as they were, are
(as, say, a small saint's obscure passion)
                                                             his
and done for the doing, favor or heaven, or no.
Then let him alone, you; he could give over
this and the next world, and without such questions,

and as you fear his music, fear him, praise
and, silent, hallow Boccherini, dead.

SOLOMON GRUNDY

A Bedtime Poem for my son

I

Pity and terror are not for little boys
who neither want nor need nor can enjoy
the agonies of Job, the blind tears
of Oedipus, or Hamlet sung to rest by angels.
Let us rehearse the tale of a good man
who lived and died in virtue and some fame,
whose tame and common truth is smooth with telling,
yet hard and fast as ever truth was told.

Solomon Grundy was born, thereafter christened,
and married in due course. Some years went by
and Mr. Grundy, husband, Christian, man
took ill, was worse in sickness, and he died.
His people laid him in earth; his epitaph
was simple: *this is the end of Solomon Grundy.*

II

We know little of him. These few events
of which we do have evidence tell nothing.
His life, like Shakespeare's, stands in bas-relief:
birth, christening, marriage, death, and stone.
No evil that he did lives after him,
and yet is remembered. Although no
records tell of any title, office,
commission, honor, real property,
nor court reports make mention of his business,
small children say his rime and bounce a ball
in private rhythms, (each of them his end).

Solomon Grundy, born, married and died . . .
his study is the limit of our knowing,
who read ourselves in him: a name in time.

III

He lived the days of the week that are our days;
his face is with the faces on our mantel
and in our albums, in dated, formal poses,
monuments to our passing.   Born on Monday,
married and the date engraved in gold . . .
as if, by such devices, we could claim
the date itself, capture the day as ours
on calendars, in almanacs, forever.

Solomon Grundy was buried on Sunday—the children,
all the endless children say it, smiling,
who know the ends of rimes and weeks and men,
simple as that. And mourn for none of them.

IV

Your eyes have closed and at the edge of sleep
you hear my voice, cozy as a blanket,
ramble on in the dark with a grim tale
of sickness and inexorable death
which you find full of symmetry and rhythm
and comforting.   When Mr. Grundy died,
that Saturday with all his days commingled
like my words now into one afternoon,
a texture on his bed, a monotone,
he knew this was no tale for a little boy
with scenes arranged around a catafalque
showing us mortal men and full of death,
nor for a father, either, whose deep voice
has lost the sing-song tune.   But you and I
must meet in the confusion of his sunset
the boundary of time and its own verge.